**Some reader re**

"Low is hardly the word for these abysmal confessions."
— *Henry James*

"Completely inappropriate for polite society."
— *Jane Austen*

"A rollicking comedy full of droll insights and effervescent obscenities." — *Marie Antoinette*

"The most unedifying book I have ever refused to finish."
— *Queen Victoria*

"A sentimental journey into the muck of Duncan's mire."
— *Henry David Thoreau*

By my fey, these lads are full on lyve—in sooth, the kynde of wights me like to swyve." — *The Wife of Bath*

"Auntie Em wouldn't let me read it." — *Dorothy*

"These low crimes and misdemeanors made me want to puke." — *Wyatt Earp*

"A bunch of stupid high-jinks that ain't worth the name of misdemeanors, much less crime." — *John Dillinger*

"A must-read for illiterates." — *George Bernard Shaw*

"Instead of the conventional *kitsch* of uplift, a puerile descent into the clamorous urges of the id."
— *Sigmund Freud*

"A stinking stewpot of sordid miscellanies. Fie upon it! Fie, I say!" — *Polonius*

"A perfect waste of time and money." — *J. P. Morgan*

"Is dribble is drubble is drabble is drovel is rub-a-flub-dub plied on with riverrun grovel." — *James Joyce*

"These tales are not for the squeamish or the faint-hearted or the intelligent. We loved 'em!" — *Larry, Curly, Moe*

# LOW CRIMES AND MISDEMEANORS

## Confessions of a Tulsa Boy

Jeff Duncan

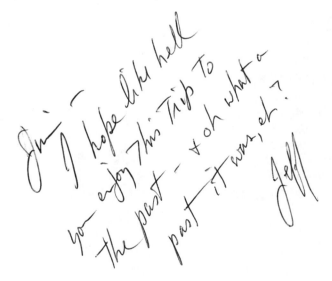

Copyright © 2009 by Jeff Duncan

*All rights reserved. No part of this book shall be reproduced or transmitted in any form or by any means, electronic, mechanical, magnetic, photographic including photocopying, recording or by any information storage and retrieval system, without prior written permission of the publisher. No patent liability is assumed with respect to the use of the information contained herein. Although every precaution has been taken in the preparation of this book, the publisher and author assume no responsibility for errors or omissions. Neither is any liability assumed for damages resulting from the use of the information contained herein.*

ISBN 0-7414-5570-6

Published by:

1094 New DeHaven Street, Suite 100
West Conshohocken, PA 19428-2713
Info@buybooksontheweb.com
www.buybooksontheweb.com
Toll-free (877) BUY BOOK
Local Phone (610) 941-9999
Fax (610) 941-9959

Printed in the United States of America
Published November 2009

*For my kids: Aly, Annie, David, Hayley, John, and Tyler.*

*For my wife Barb.*

*For my old Tulsa buddies.*

*And for Mom.*

# PREFACE

For years my sons and daughters have urged me to write down my memories of growing up in Oklahoma in the forties and fifties. They've especially wanted me to write about the messes and mischief and trouble that my buddies and I made and got into, and that got into us—so they can have a sense of what their old man was like growing up a rowdy kid in a rowdy time and place, so far removed from the married, home-owning, tax-paying, ballot-casting, child-rearing, church-going English professor they're familiar with. And now that all of them are grown up and know better than to take me in my youth as some sort of role model, I have obliged them.

But I have written this memoir for a general audience as well. (Except for kids: this is *not* a book for kids.) I think most of us find growing-up stories interesting, even fascinating, for two reasons. First, such stories have the hook of familiarity: *we* have grown up, been there, done that. We can identify. At the same time, such stories have the hook of unfamiliarity: we grow up in different times and places, in worlds that to others are often remote, strange, even exotic. As for trouble, that's what stories are all about.

So here it is, a collection of reminiscences about my childhood and adolescence. I have arranged them in roughly chronological order, starting with the earliest in 1943 or so and ending with high school graduation in 1957, when I moved from Oklahoma never to live there again, only to visit now and then. In my mind and heart, though, I visit there all the time, and now you may, if you like, visit with me.

(For the record, I have changed a number of names, to protect the innocent *and* the guilty.)

Ann Arbor, 2009

## Playing with Fire

When I was four years old I became fascinated with fire. I struck matches whenever I found any. I loved the initial flare, then the flame which you could make bigger or smaller by turning the match up or down. To make me stop, my mother tried smacking me with her hand, spanking me with a paddle, and whipping me with a belt, but to no avail. One evening she caught me striking them yet again, and, as both of us screamed and cried, she seared my fingers in the flame of the kitchen stove. Her fury and desperation are understandable: one day I had set the yard behind us on fire, and she was terrified that I would do the same to our house. So she burned me, hoping that the pain of fire would stop me from playing with fire. It didn't.

Finally Mom admitted defeat and went to a child psychologist (she told me years later). He had a suggestion.

On a bright sunny morning, perfect for playing outdoors, she set me down on the kitchen floor with a brand new box of kitchen matches. Diamond, red tip. Then she told me to strike them, one by one, and let them burn down almost to my fingertips before blowing them out. At first I couldn't believe my luck, but by the time I was a third of the way through the box I had had enough. Too bad, she said: I had to strike every single one. I tried cheating—tried blowing them out sooner, tried hiding them under my legs, in my pockets—but I couldn't get away with anything. Mom was there, watching, the whole time. And the time slid slowly, like lukewarm tar down the side of a bucket. I could hear my pals outside, playing. I could hear the clock inside, ticking. My back ached. My legs ached. My butt ached. I complained and pleaded, but Mom had no mercy: I had to keep striking them, one after another.

When I finished, it was dinner time. The whole day shot. I never played with fire again.

Not literally, anyway.

## A Warning

It was midmorning of a warm autumn day, the sky bright blue, the leaves red, orange, yellow, brown. Many leaves had fallen, littering yards, driveways, sidewalks, the street. I was knocking around by myself. Everyone else was in school. I wasn't old enough for school yet. For some reason—nothing else to do, I guess—I started kicking the leaves in the street along the curb down toward the corner. A few leaves became many, and the many multiplied into a good sized pile. It seemed to grow of its own accord, magically, like the little pot that boiled out porridge. By the time I got down to the corner, my pile of leaves was thigh high.

I didn't know what to do with them, but I felt I had to do something. I couldn't just leave them there. I wanted some kind of closure. So I stuffed them into the sewer.

Two or three days later while I was hacking around in the front yard, I saw a city truck pull up to the corner. Two men got out, looked at the sewer, then lifted the grate and started raking the leaves out. Theoretically speaking, I could have stayed in my yard, keeping my distance, but practically speaking I couldn't. I had to go there. Didn't know why, but had to.

I crossed the street and slowly moseyed down the sidewalk with my hands in my pockets, trying to look real casual, just an innocent pedestrian passing by. I was probably even whistling. But I couldn't pass by. I had to stop, and watch them. My mouth was dry, my chest tight, my heart hammering with anxiety. With guilt. With terror.

The men looked up from their work. "You know who did this?" one of them asked.

"No sir."

"If it rains with the sewer all stopped up like it was, you know what'd happen?"

"No sir."

"It'd flood!" number two man said. "All these homes'd git swept away. People and their pets git drownded."

"Oh."

"You want people and pets to git drownded?" number one asked.

"No sir."

"Course not," number two said, "so if you ever find out who did it, you tell that sonofabitch if he ever does it again, he'll go to jail. Might never git out. You understand?"

"Yes sir."

"Good," the first man said. "Now git on back home and mind your mama."

"Yes sir."

I went back home. Mom asked me what the men were doing. I said they were cleaning out the sewer. I didn't go into detail. But I sort of took the men's advice. I never stuffed leaves into a sewer again. As for minding my mama, well, that depended....

## Scraps

Whether it's still true or not, in the Oklahoma of my childhood, boys were expected to fight. Or at least they were in my neighborhood. The price for declining to fight was steep: scorn, ostracism, disgrace. So, wanting and liking to think of myself as tough, I got into scraps now and then.

The first I remember was when I was five or so. Billy Wall and I saw a long piece of rope in the street and grabbed for it at the same time. Billy was a neighborhood pal, but friendship didn't keep us from fighting over that rope, pushing, pulling, and hitting each other, starting in the street, then on into my yard, and then up the steps onto my front porch, where Mom watched and officiated. ("No kicking, Jeffrey," she warned. "Above the belt, Billy; above the belt.") Somehow Billy got the rope around my neck, whereupon he yanked it hard, tore it out of my grasp, and took off. So he got the rope, but I got a rope burn on the side of my neck, a battle wound that I showed off to everybody, including Billy, as if it were a medal.

The boy next door, Jimmy Riskoski, was a couple of years older than me. We usually went our separate ways, but occasionally we played together. One time we got into a huge fight. I don't remember what it was about, but I do remember that it covered three back yards and that we were thumping each other pretty good, and that I was happily surprised to be holding my own. Then Jimmy kicked me in the balls and I went down. So I could claim a moral victory of sorts—Jimmy had to cheat to whip me—but I learned that moral victories have their limits: my balls really hurt.

A kid named Bobby Carl lived several houses up the street. One day we were hanging around together and he found a cigar butt on the sidewalk. He picked it up, stuck it in his mouth, and swaggered around like a big shot mobster in the movies. He was really funny. I envied Bobby, because I liked being funny and wished that *I* had found the butt and stuck it in *my* mouth and swaggered around like Jimmy Cagney. When his mother called him in for lunch, I decided to get even by blurting, "Bobby had a cigar in his mouth!" He punched me in the stomach, hard, and his mother said, "Don't be a tattle-tale, Jeffrey."

"Yes'm," I wheezed. Ordinarily I would have fought back, but this time I didn't deserve to: I knew I had broken a serious taboo—my sense of shame told me so—and I had been properly chastised and punished for it.

One summer morning I saw Jimmy Riskoski, Bobby Carl, Billy and Tommy Wall (Billy's older brother) walk off together. I joined them. I had no idea where they—now we—were going. We walked to an alley behind some stores a couple of blocks away on Admiral Street and saw several guys I had never seen before. Jimmy and Tommy swapped insults with them, and soon we were throwing rocks at each other.

I saw one of the other guys hurl a good sized one. I watched it as it rose into the air, as it peaked, then as it descended straight toward me. I had learned somewhere that when a missile is coming toward you, you should duck, so I did. Unfortunately, I miscalculated its trajectory and it landed right on top of my head. It drew blood and raised a knot, but instead of feeling proud of my war wound, the way I did with the rope burn, I felt stupid. I wore a hat for a couple of weeks, to hide it.

One chilly autumn afternoon a bunch of us neighborhood boys—Billy and Tommy Wall, Jimmy Riskoski, Bobby Carl, Bobby Duvall, Johnny Warnken, David Woolsey, Paul Moser, and I—were aimlessly hanging around the vacant lot across the street from the Walls. The lot was a mess—big holes and piles of dirt here and there, and litter of all sorts everywhere: empty cardboard cartons, empty pop and beer and whiskey bottles, candy wrappers, potato chip and Frito bags, rubbers, and the like. One guy threw a used Kotex napkin at another. The throw-ee hurled a dirt clod back at the throw-er, and immediately we fell into two groups throwing dirt clods and rocks at each other. One group took cover behind a couple of dirt piles, popping up now and then to fire off a salvo. The other group, the one I was in, stayed out in the open, using cardboard boxes as shields. It was a friendly fight, but we were throwing as hard as we could. When we got hit we laughed along with everyone else, in spite of—and also because of—the pain. We battled until it was too dark to see, then hustled home, our spirits bursting with adrenalin.

### Springshoes

As soon as I could read, Mom got me a subscription to a magazine called *Children's Activities.* Out of all the articles and puzzles and pictures, what impressed me most was Johnny Springshoes. He was the hero of a cartoon strip selling springshoes: two shoe-shaped plates of steel, one at the bottom, the other at the top of two coiled springs, one spring at the heel, the other at the ball of the foot. The top plate had a toe strap and an ankle strap, like the roller skates of the day. Wearing his springshoes, Johnny did all sorts of wonderful things: he bounced up into tree branches to fetch stranded kittens, bounced over fences to apprehend crooks, bounced up to second story windows to rescue babies from burning buildings. I mean, with springshoes you could damn near fly, whereas with Keds and P.F. Flyers you could only run faster'n hell. I just had to have me a pair. No one else did—I'd be the hero of the neighborhood. Mom said that if I could get the money together, three ninety-five plus postage, she'd order them.

In 1945 three ninety-five was a fortune for a first-grader. I had two ways to raise money. One was to rifle the couch and chairs and drawers for loose change. The other was to take empty pop bottles to the grocery store for the refund: two cents a bottle. Mom didn't buy pop, so the only way I could get bottles was to scrounge around for them in alleys and vacant lots.

It took I don't know how many months, but I did it. Mom sent in the order and several weeks later my spring-shoes finally arrived.

I ripped open the box, pulled out the shoes. They were dazzling. The steel plates were nickel colored, the straps and three-inch springs red. By this time all the kids in the neighborhood had come to see. Some of their parents too. I strapped the shoes on, stood up and wobbled to the edge of the porch. From the porch to the ground was only about a two-foot drop, not enough, I figured, to bounce up into the maple in our yard, but certainly out to the sidewalk. "Well, here goes, everbody—Geronimo!" I hollered, and jumped. Instead of bouncing, though, I instantly fell in a heap, my ankles sprained, my hopes, expectations, and ego broken. As everyone laughed I took the springshoes off and managed to stand up and hobble into the house, pretending to be as amused as they were, though it was all I could do not to cry in pain and disappointment.

A few weeks later, when my ankles and ego had healed, I tried the shoes again, though much more cautiously this time, the way you pet a horse that bites. I didn't sprain my ankles, and eventually I learned to lope along in a springing boinging gait a bit like Tigger's. I got a lot of laughs, but I never did bounce and soar over fences or onto rooftops apprehending crooks or into trees saving kittens, and I never did buy anything mail order again, either.

## A Swimming Lesson

When I was seven Mom enrolled me in the YMCA, an old red brick building on the corner of Fourth and Cincinnati, downtown. We had no car, so I took the bus. I went by myself. (Tulsa was safe, but even so, I was the only seven-year old I knew whose mother let him go downtown by himself.) I wandered around the facility watching the kids shooting pool, playing ping-pong and basketball, horsing around on gymnastics equipment. Then we were summoned to go swimming. The other guys seemed to know what they were doing, so I followed them.

After stripping and showering we lined up butt-naked along the length of the pool. I had never seen a swimming pool before. I was intrigued by the swish and shimmer of the blue-green water and its reflection off the ceiling and walls, and by the smell of the chlorine. A man in a bathing suit standing on the other side ordered us to count off. When the count was finished he yelled, "Okay, fall in," and all the boys leaped into the pool.

I leaped too, only to discover there was no bottom. I thrashed my legs and arms and managed to get back up to the surface, to grab a breath and try to yell "Help," but before I could get the word out I was sinking again. Again I thrashed, got back up to the surface, grabbed a breath and tried to holler "Help" but was sinking again. I managed once again to get back up, but this time instead of air I inhaled water. I was sinking in a blind panic when I felt myself being dragged up out of the pool.

I gasped and coughed and cried as two boys older and bigger than me pounded my back and said, "Sorry, kid! We'd've grabbed you sooner, but we thought you were puttin' us on."

"Huh uh," I answered.

"Didn't you know this is the deep end?"

"Huh uh."

"But there's the diving board."

After a pause I said, "Oh." That was all I said because, as improbable as this may sound, until they pointed it out I hadn't seen it, which made me feel pretty stupid, so I didn't say anything else lest I sound and look even stupider.

"Are you alright now?"

"Yeah," I said, and I actually was. I went down to the shallow end, jumped in, and had a grand time. To this day I don't know if I was sort of brave to go right back in like that, or if I really was just stupid.

### Crime and Punishment

One summer morning my mom's mom, Gram, was looking after my younger brother Chris and me. She had a doctor's appointment at noon, and she told us, DO NOT WANDER OFF.

I was playing ball two blocks away on Harwell Field—where Tulsa University's baseball and football teams practiced and the neighborhood boys played—when I heard Gram holler, "JEFFREY LIGHT!" She was standing in the middle of the street. "COME HERE RIGHT NOW!" Answering, "Yes ma'am!" ("Jeffrey Light" meant I was in deep deep trouble), I ran to her. "I told you not to wander off!" she yelled, and slapped me across the face. "Where's your brother!"

"Up the alley pickin' grapes," I said, trying not to cry.

"Go get him!"

"Yes'm," I said. I ran to the alley and hollered, "CHRIS! C'MERE, QUICK! GRAM WANTS YOU!"

He and Gram got to where I was standing at the same time. "I told you not to wander off!" she yelled at him, then grabbed us both by the backs of our shirts.

"Hey!" I protested. "You slapped me! How come you didn't slap Chris!"

Now, you have to understand that while I was big for my age, Chris was little. Very little. He was not only second-born and small, however; he was also visited with serious afflictions from the get-go. He arrived in this world feet-first a month early. He got pneumonia when he was a few weeks old and barely survived. When he started walking he had to wear a truss for the hernia he was born with. At the age of two he had to start wearing glasses. When he was seven or eight he had his tonsils taken out, but instead of the ordinary in-one-day-out-the-next procedure, he stayed in the hospital for a week getting a penicillin shot in his bum six times a day to quell the infection he had somehow sustained. His cheeks looked like a couple of pin cushions. A year or two later he had eye surgery, to correct a muscular disorder that made him cockeyed. A year or two after that he had foot surgery, to bring his little toes down to ground level and thus improve his balance. Later on still, when he was eighteen, he had heart surgery, to replace a defective valve. So Chris got a lot of sympathy, and for good reason, but I often resented it anyway. Especially that morning when my face was still stinging and my heart was sore. So I protested, "How come you didn't slap Chris!"

Whereupon Gram hauled back and slapped me again, saying, "Mind your own business!" Then she grabbed us by the backs of our shirts again and, holding us like a couple of string-puppets, hauled us to the alley, down the alley and through the gate into the yard and through the side door into the garage. "Take off your shirts!" she ordered. Without a word—Chris and I had learned our lesson: we weren't gonna say shit—we took off our shirts. Then she grabbed a switch from the workbench, where, I now noticed, there were two bunches of switches, with about twenty in each bunch, and I thought to myself, *Uh oh.*

She laid into my back until she had broken every switch in one bunch, then she did the same to Chris with the other. Our backs were laced with scratches. She washed our backs and sent us to bed for the rest of the afternoon, until dinner.

A few years ago Aunt Jeanne (Mom's sister) and Uncle Earle asked me to tell that story again, and after they had finished laughing they asked if Gram had ever talked to me about that day. I said no. Probably couldn't, they said: she was consumed with remorse and guilt about it the rest of her life.

I had no idea. I had no idea, not only because she never told me, but also because it never occurred to me that she would or should feel remorseful or guilty. *Chris and I* were the ones who'd done wrong. We had only gotten what was coming to us. To our whole family (with the exception of Gram, sad to say), the episode was the stuff of comedy.

I wish she had said something, so I could have put my arms around her and told her it was okay. It was okay even when it happened. Better than okay: as I bragged to all my buddies while showing off my scratches, not many boys get a whuppin' like that.

### Learning a Hard Way

When I was eight years old, Gram and my grandfather Grad, wanting the kind of life they grew up in back in southern Illinois, sold their house in Tulsa to Mom (she divorced my dad when I was like six) and moved to Pauls Valley, a small town about sixty miles south of Oklahoma City. Their first year they rented a big old wood-frame farm house that came with a large garage, a barn in a state of near collapse, and numerous pecan trees, all on a lot that took up a city block. The house had once been grand: high ceilings, tall double-hung windows, a large living room on one side of the entry hall, and on the other side a real, honest-to-God parlor. Now the house was ramshackle and drafty and remarkably comfortable.

It was located in the white slums, across Highway 19 from the black slums (or colored town, as we used to say), and behind a high bank of the Washita River. I never went across the highway into colored town—no whites did, to my knowledge—nor did I ever see any colored cross to our side. I didn't cross the street into the white slums, either. I kept my distance because, for the first and only time in my life, I was the rich kid in the neighborhood, and I knew, subliminally but certainly, that I wouldn't be welcome. Not that we were rich, but those folks were *poor*. The first time I visited was Thanksgiving, and those kids were still barefoot. At Christmas many still were. They knocked on the door now and then looking for odd jobs to make some money—rake and burn the leaves, pick pecans, clean up whatever might need cleaning up—but other than that they kept their distance. They were almost as strange to me as the colored were. They lived in two-room unpainted shacks perched on cinder blocks with no sidewalks, no grassy lawns, and no order to their placement—a different world.

The summer of my ninth year, Chris and I stayed with Gram and Grad for a few weeks. I was pretty much on my own. Chris and I never played together much. He wasn't athletic, so catch and basketball were out of the picture. We both read a lot, but we didn't read *together*, you know? Going across the street to play with the neighborhood kids didn't even occur to me. So I spent a lot of time shooting marbles, spinning a top in the street, throwing a tennis ball against the side of the garage to work on grounders, shooting at the basket over the garage door, and throwing a lariat at fence posts as I galloped by them like a cowboy on horseback. I got better at picking up grounders and sinking shots, but I never got anywhere roping fence posts. I was not, I concluded, cowboy material.

My main chore that summer was to keep the yard mowed. It was a large yard. Two sides were under trees, so the grass was thin and easy to cut. The other two sides, however, had a lot of exposure to the sun, so the grass grew thick. Worse yet, it was Bermuda grass, which is popular in that part of the country because it can take a lot of heat, but it is coarse, heavy, hard to cut, and I had to use a push mower. So, even though I got paid for it, I'd mow only a few swaths, then go read or shoot some baskets or practice fielding grounders. In the afternoon Chris and I would often walk downtown to see a movie. Next day I'd remember my mowing job, or Gram would remind me, and I'd cut a few more swaths, then pack it in.

One late afternoon, when Chris and I got back to the house from a double-feature, I saw two eleven or twelve year old boys from across the street mowing the yard. Oddly, a pang of jealousy cramped my chest. My ego could hardly catch its breath. Okay, I had slacked off, but still, these guys were mowing *my* yard, doing *my* job. I approached them and asked one of those questions that's so mindless you immediately regret asking it: "Whatch yall doin'?"

"Whadda you think?" one of them said: "We're mowin' this here grass."

"Oh."

"The lady here has a grandkid who's supposed to," the other said, "but he's lazy as hell and just won't do it."

"So we got the job. And she pays good too."

"Real good."

"Oh."

"That kid ain't just lazy, man. He's fuckin' stupid!"

"Oh."

I walked into the house feeling like a dumbbell. I didn't say anything, nor did Gram or Grad, but after that day I mowed the yard.

Need I say that Gram had set me up? Paid those boys

a bonus to say what they did, she told me years later. She knew my buttons.

### *Brotherly Differences*

In our front yard one Sunday evening, Johnny Johnson and I were playing Perry and Charles Mahan for the East Fourth Place Croquet Doubles Championship of the Day. Johnny and I had gotten way behind, but then staged a remarkable comeback and won. Hollering, "Yee-haaw!" I swung my mallet around as hard as I could and hit Chris right in the middle of his forehead, maybe an inch above his glasses. He staggered back a few steps but somehow didn't fall down. Then he bellowed and I screamed for Mom. She came charging out of the house. We helped him inside, sat him down on the couch. I made an icepack. Mom held it against his head and stroked him and made sure he didn't go to sleep. I apologized and explained I had no idea he was standing right behind me. They knew that. I felt like crud anyway.

First thing next morning, Mom and I took Chris to our family physician, Dr. Reed. He said that, amazingly, Chris didn't have a concussion. He also said that if I had hit him a little lower I would have broken his nose; a little lower and a little to either side I would have put out one eye or the other; on the side of his head, in the temple, I well could have killed him. But I had still done some serious damage: Chris had an enormous goose egg, and both of his eyes blacked and blued and yellowed to the bottom of his cheeks. His face looked like a self-portrait of a German Expressionist painted in a fit of self-loathing. It took weeks to heal. Until it healed, I treated Chris much better than usual, with consideration, even tenderness.

But I wasn't usually nice to Chris. Since he was the little brother who really was little and who had all those ailments needing repair one after the other, Mom raised him very differently from the way she raised me. Me she raised to be self-reliant; him she coddled. So I'm sure I mistreated Chris at times because I was jealous, but not always, because I *liked* to think of myself as being independent, manly, tough, and Chris, as far as I was concerned, was babyish. But that was why he often aggravated me. One morning, for example, he was sitting in a chair staring into space sniveling and crying, as he often did. After a while I demanded, "What's the matter?"

"My sock," he said.

"What's wrong with your sock?"

"It's got a hole in it," he cried.

"You're crying on account of a hole in your sock!" I hollered. "I'll give you something to cry about!" and I smacked his head a few times, until Mom told me to leave him alone as she fetched him a pair without blemish.

Things like that.

One time he stayed home sick. Mom had gone to work, I was running late and asked him if he would make me a sandwich for lunch. He said sure. Come lunch time I took a bite and almost puked on the spot. I opened it up and saw that the lettuce was brown and slimy. In a rage, I ran home—a good half-a-mile—and yelled, "Why did you put rotten lettuce in my sandwich!"

"I didn't know it was rotten!"

"How could you *not* know! It's brown and slimy!"

"I don't know! I just didn't notice!"

"Didn't notice!" I hollered. "Well I bet you'll notice this!" and I hit him in the head a few times, then shoved the sandwich in his mouth. I grabbed some bread and lunchmeat and ate them on the run back to school.

But I insisted on having hope for Chris. When he was nine or ten I decided he could be an athlete, like me. Basketball and football were out of the question—he was too little—so I decided to make him a baseball player. I got him a glove and forced him to practice in our backyard and at T.U. After a year Chris had gotten pretty good at fielding grounders as long as they weren't coming too hard, but he still couldn't catch high flies or hit worth crap. The reason was simple: he was afraid of the ball. I finally gave up, deeming him a hopeless candy-ass.

(Later, when he had an eye operation, I found out he had no depth perception. So no wonder he was afraid of the ball!—when you can't tell how far away it is or how fast it's coming, you've got reason to be afraid.)

One summer weekday Chris and I were returning from T.U. where I had been working him on his hitting. It hadn't gone well. We weren't speaking. At the top of the alley—which was a bumpy grass-and-dirt affair, like a little-used country lane—I said, "Race you home," and took off. Chris didn't even run. He had no chance and he knew it. I pushed the gate open and walked through, then pushed the gate shut. I walked into the kitchen, drank a glass of water, and went to the bedroom we shared to look at *Sport* magazine. Chris had disappeared from my mind.

Then I heard him start bellowing, so loud you could hear him in the next block. "GODDAMN SON OF A BITCH! FUCKIN' ASSHOLE! NO GOOD BASTARD SHITFACE COCKSUCKER!" Etc. I looked out the window. He was still in the alley, a little loud knot of fury jumping up and down struggling to open the gate. It hadn't occurred to me that he would have trouble opening it. That wasn't the reason I had closed it. I had closed it because I always closed it, so our pet duck Dinah couldn't get out. But the sight and sound of him hopping and bellowing in an obscenity-riddled rage struck me as outrageously funny. I fell on my bed I was laughing so hard.

Soon I realized that Chris had stopped bellowing. Silence. A strange silence. Then I heard him again, though now his voice was a hoarse, raspy, menacing snarl. "Whar is he!" He was in the house. "Whar is that no-good low-life sonofabitch!" He was approaching our bedroom. "Ah'm gonna kill the dirty, no-good motherfucker!" Then he appeared in the doorway.

His face was the color of a red onion, the blue veins in his temples pulsing, his blue eyes watery and wild. He was wielding a butcher knife. "Ah'm gonna slice your god-damned gizzard out!" I was laughing, even though I knew he meant it. No, I was laughing *because* he meant it. It was like being threatened by a berserk Pomeranian. He snarled, "Laugh at THIS, cocksucker!" and leaped toward me slashing the knife. Still laughing, I managed to dodge him. He leaped and slashed again, and I dodged him again. I couldn't stop laughing, even though it made dodging difficult, but the very real danger made the situation even crazier, even funnier.

We did this wild dance all over our bedroom until I finally managed to stop laughing and disarm him, about as quick as that. Which made him even madder, but I held him tight in a bear hug from behind and insisted that I hadn't intended to shut him out of the yard. After a while he quit thrashing and cursing and I let him go. Then, as usual, he went his way and I went mine.

Chris wanted to cut me up, but what he really wanted, I now understand, was to get some respect. That's what he always wanted—just a little respect. And most of the time I didn't have it in my heart to give him any.

### My Colored Buddy

Gram and Grad had a maid, Dolly, who came to clean their house once a week. When they moved to Pauls Valley and we lived in that house—the house that they built and that Mom grew up in—Dolly started working for us. She came every other week at most, because Mom couldn't afford any more than that. I was curious about Dolly, about what it was like to be colored, to be poor, to live in a shack on a tree-lined dirt lane crammed with other shacks and crowded with people, but I didn't know how to ask her such questions. So I asked Mom, and she told me what she knew, which included the following: a few years before, Dolly had left Tulsa to marry a man in Wichita, Kansas, and while she was gone Gram hired a woman named Marie who, like Mom, had two sons the same age as Chris and me.

Now I don't know why, but this colored woman Marie and her two nameless sons stuck to my mind. I was sure she was as pretty as Mom, and I was equally sure her son my age was into sports and was a lot of fun to hang around with, and wouldn't that be neat, to have a colored buddy to play basketball and football and baseball with? I didn't talk to him as if he were by my side or anything like that—my imagination has never been that vivid—but he was a presence in my mind, like a memory, like an image you form of a person from a voice.

One day the art teacher told us to draw the face of our best friend. I drew a generic boy's face, then, not really thinking but just letting fantasy have its way, I colored it in with a black crayon. When she saw it, the teacher gasped. "That's your friend?" she asked. As soon as she asked I realized I had drawn a wish rather than a reality, but I didn't want to admit it.

"Yes ma'am."

"You have a colored boy for a friend?"

"Yes ma'am."

"Where do you know him from?"

"Well, his mama cleans our house, and when she comes over she brings him with her, and we play catch and marbles and tag and follow-the-leader and crack-the-whip and things like that." My imagination was beginning to peter out—two boys make for a very short whip—so I was hoping she wouldn't ask me any more questions, but she did.

"What's his name?"

My mind went blank, then in a panic my mouth blurted, "Rastus."

It was the first name that came to mind, and it couldn't have been worse: Rastus was the stock name of every nigger joke I'd ever heard. And, accordingly, she laughed, but she wasn't happy. She took me to the principal's office, showed him my portrait, and told him my story. He asked me if it was true. I insisted it was. He called Mom and asked the same question. As I gauged from his responses, Mom said it wasn't. Mightily relieved, the principal assured the teacher everything was alright, then told me I shouldn't tell stories, especially stories like that, and she and I returned to class.

Thereafter I refrained from stories like that. But I still thought it would be really, really neat if that colored boy and I were buddies.

### *A Stranger of Sorts in a Strange Land*

One day, when I was ten or so, Gram, for a reason I don't know, took me and our black Cocker Spaniel to Ardmore, a town about sixty miles south of Pauls Valley. As soon as Gram pulled into a diagonal parking slot on downtown Main Street, the dog jumped out of the car and took off. Gram and I split up, she combing one side of the street, I the other.

I felt foolish walking along the sidewalk and entering stores one by one calling our dog. Had she been named something like Blackie or Muffin, it wouldn't have been so bad, but Barbara? As I called her name and made smooching sounds with my lips, people looked at me with the condescending smiles I didn't want. I came out of T.G.&Y.—a large chain of dime stores—and was walking down the sidewalk calling and looking left and right when I saw a guy about my age approaching. He looked vaguely familiar, which struck me as odd because I'd never been to Ardmore before and it was a long way from Tulsa, so what a coincidence, running into an acquaintance two hundred miles from home. I was trying to figure out who he could be without staring, which would be rude, and besides, I had to keep my eye out for Barbara, so I slipped in furtive little glances now and then, but still couldn't identify him.

Then I noticed he seemed to be walking towards me—directly towards me—and I wondered if he was challenging me or something. I continued looking and calling for Barbara and quickly glancing at this guy, not only to figure out who he might be, but also to see if he really was walking towards me, and I had to conclude that sure enough he was. He was actually challenging me to a game of chicken. So I had to decide how to respond: to step aside, acknowledging thereby that I *was* a chicken? Or to walk straight ahead myself and make him—or me!—suffer the consequences? Honor was on the line. There was hardly anything worse in the Oklahoma of my childhood than being a chicken. The proper thing to do was clear. "Fuck him," I thought, looked the sonofabitch right in the eye, braced myself, and walked face-first into a mirror.

I was embarrassed and confused. It was a kind of identity crisis, after all: whether in some ultimate sense we are our bodies or not, the fact was that I hadn't recognized myself. But I wasn't so confused that I didn't look around to see if anyone had seen me walk smack into a mirror. Luckily, no one had.

I have no idea how or where we found the damn dog.

### Hunting Fowl

Gram and Grad moved into a new house right on the line between town and country. In front of their house: Pauls Valley. Behind it: corn fields. So they let me have what they wouldn't let me have before and that I couldn't have in Tulsa: a BB gun. It was a Daisy carbine. It looked like it belonged in a saddle holster—very western, very neat.

From the back porch and the patio I worked on becoming a marksman, aiming at anything that could serve as a target: the telephone pole, a wheelbarrow, a bucket, tin cans, bottles, a pansy here, a petunia there. I noticed that my Daisy didn't shoot true—I could see the glint of the copper BB hooking to the left—so I practiced compensating for its errant path. After a couple of weeks I decided the time had come for the real thing—to hunt for game.

I took off in the morning through the corn fields for the Washita River, about a mile away. It meandered through quicksand and grassy banks dotted here and there with a small tree or two. I found a sapling that would be perfect—it was dead, leafless. A bird would be completely exposed. I positioned myself in a nearby clump of tall Johnson grass and silently, motionlessly waited for one to land. One finally did—a blue jay

I slowly raised my rifle to my shoulder, took aim, fired, and saw the glint of the BB flash past the jay to his right. I carefully, quietly pumped the lever, took aim again, fired, and saw the glint of the BB flash past him to his left. Next I shot over him, then under. And all the while he was looking right at me with an expression of studied indifference, as if he somehow knew that even though I was only twelve feet away, I was no threat and he was in no danger. And he was right. I fired again and again, until after a while he flew off, probably to see if he could find some other kid with a BB gun who could give him a little excitement.

Disappointed, frustrated, I was trudging back to the house when I had this idea. There was a barnyard near Gram and Grad's. And in that yard there were some chickens. Chickens were a lot bigger than blue jays—maybe I could hit one of them. So I walked to the barnyard. A number of chickens were pecking around. No person was in sight. I took aim at the nearest hen and fired. With a mighty squawk she shot straight up into the air a good ten feet, her neck outstretched and her beak wide open, her wings flapping and her feathers flying, just like the cartoons. She landed, shook her tail in a huff, then resumed pecking around for bugs and stray bits of grain. I walked back to the house feeling much improved.

## *Johnny*

My best buddy was Johnny Nilson. We started hanging around with each other when we were ten. Johnny was cute. Brown tousled hair. Big brown eyes with thick, long lashes. A quick sense of humor and a great big toothy smile. Good manners yet ornery, just the way my mother and her female friends liked a boy to be—Tom Sawyer in the flesh.

Johnny's family had more money than his friends' families, which meant that Johnny usually had more than his friends did. When a group of us would agree to pool all our money for this purpose or that, Johnny would secretly hold out, having a five or a ten tightly folded up and squirreled away somewhere on his person or in his wallet. Sometimes that extra came in handy, to bale us out of a sticky situation (a bus fare, an admission fee, some gas), but it irritated the hell out of us anyway. The principle of the thing. But we forgave him.

One time several of us were spending the day at the Y and got hungry. Only Johnny had any money. We asked if he'd lend us some to buy a sandwich. He said sure, but then refused to lend us the thirty cents we wanted for a barbecue sandwich, because he was going to spend only twenty-five for a hamburger. "It's just a nickel!" we protested. "A quarter," he said: "take it or leave it." Seething, we took it, and a little later forgave him.

Playing games—Monopoly, parcheesi, Old Maid, ping-pong, horse-shoes, croquet, you name it—he would cheat just to see if he could get away with it. When we caught him he'd laugh and say, "What're yall gittin' so hot and bothered about? It's just a game." And we forgave him.

We always forgave him because he was so much fun. In fifth grade he and I worked at the cafeteria during lunch. The job got us out of some class time, got us a free lunch, and got us an opportunity to play the fool. We would sashay around with plates balanced on our heads while singing, "There's a place in France / where the ladies do a dance, / and the dance they do / is the kitchy kitchy koo," and we would kick in unison like chorus girls. Sometimes we'd lose the plate. We also broke dishes by tossing them to each other, making behind-the-back and under-the-leg passes.

We especially liked taking the dishes as the kids handed them in. With apt commentary and sound effects, we would smear leftover peas and carrots with our fists and palms, squeeze jello and pudding through our fingers, stir various scraps in a bowl to look like vomit, dip our hands in chili then hold them out and invite one and all to have a smell of diarrhea. They would groan and laugh, and Johnny and I would do an encore.

The following year I was appointed Captain of the Safety Patrols (don't ask me how: I haven't the vaguest memory or idea) and I immediately appointed Johnny as my lieutenant. He requested cafeteria duty. I asked why. He said I'd see. And I did. At the cafeteria his job was to check all the kids at the exit to make sure they didn't carry any food out to the playground. According to the job description, anyway. What Johnny actually did was shake the kids down. For half of what they had, he'd let them carry the other half on out. At the end of lunch hour, he would split the take with me, supposedly fifty-fifty, but given Johnny's ways and means, I'd wager it was more like sixty-forty. At afternoon recess and after school we would sell our take: a few Oreos, Milk Duds, Hershey's Kisses; halves of Milky Ways, Baby Ruths, Snickers, Mars Bars, Butterfingers; some sticks of Spearmint and Juicy Fruit and pieces of Fleer's Double Bubble. Since we had no overhead or debt, and since we didn't even pay wholesale, and since we weren't greedy, we offered bargains—a penny a unit. Which was probably why no one ever ratted on us.

### Scouting

Johnny and I joined Boy Scout Troop 37 as soon as we could. We learned the easy Scouting stuff—the salute, the pledge, the motto—but we didn't bother to learn Morse code, semaphore, and all those knots that, in our estimation, only sailors of yore needed to know and who the hell was going to sail a Galleon or a Yankee Clipper in Oklahoma? Besides, we didn't join the Scouts to learn anything; we joined to go camping.

And were we lucky. The troop master, Curly Fowler, took us camping at least once a month no matter the season or the weather. We usually went somewhere near Arkansas, in the foothills of the Ozarks, rocky country laced with spring-fed creeks, but we occasionally camped at other spots as well. We left on Friday evenings and returned on Sunday afternoons. After we arrived and set up camp, Curly pretty much turned us loose. I remember winter trips when it was so cold we slept two in a sleeping bag for warmth. I remember jumping in Spring Creek in February, hiking together through the woods trying to catch or kill a critter (any critter), wading hand-in-hand across the Canadian River in quicksand, jumping off cliffs into rivers and swimming holes.

According to the principle of doing unto others what was done unto you, we took newcomers at night deep into the woods to hunt for snipe, leaving them alone to find their way back to the campsite after they finally realized there were no snipe. We played hide-and-seek and capture-the-flag in the woods. We made big bonfires and danced around the flames, and jumped over and through the flames. We scorched hotdogs and marshmallows on sticks, roasted onions and ears of corn in aluminum foil, baked potatoes in casings of mud. We ate chips and drank pop and belched and farted. We smoked grape vine and dried-out driftwood. We told dirty jokes and tall tales. We did *not* sing "Kumbaya" or "Ninety-Nine Bottles of Beer on the Wall" or any other songs you were supposed to sing at camp.

One Sunday, a gorgeous spring day—the redbuds and dogwoods in bloom, the birds in song, the sunshot air in angel mode, soft and feathery and chock full of ions—the dads told us right after lunch to pack up our gear and wash up our mess kits so we could get on back to Tulsa, which was considerably earlier than usual. I suspected they wanted to get home so they could do some yard work or play a round of golf. Near the tents there was a water faucet that all the guys lined up to use. I suggested to Johnny that we wash our mess kits in the creek instead. It would be quicker than waiting in line, and it would be more outdoorsy and authentic, like the way mountain men and pioneers and prospectors washed, with sand and gravel in rushing water rather than with a factory-made brillo pad under a twentieth-century faucet.

We hustled down to the creek, carefully arranged the pieces of our mess kits on the stony ledges of the steep, fifteen-foot bank, took off our shoes, rolled up our pants, and commenced to scrub. We were feeling pretty smug and authentic when a quick little hiccup of breeze tumbled our mess kits into the creek. For a second we watched our tin cups and bowls and plates bobbing merrily up and down the ripples and wavelets of the current, as if they were celebrating their release with a float trip. Then we yelled "Oh shit!" and took off in the knee-deep water to retrieve them.

The problem was, the creek bed was composed of small flint rocks with sharp edges. We would run a few feet, step on a particularly sharp rock and collapse into the water, scramble up, run a few more feet, hit another sharp one and collapse again. We could see the pieces of our mess kits glinting in the sunlight, floating farther and farther away. After a dozen falls or so we gave up and started walking—carefully, gingerly, delicately, sore-footedly—back upstream.

Just then we heard hollering. "Duncan! Nilson!" We looked up and saw three dads looking down at us. "What in God's name are yall doin' down there?"

"We were washin' our mess kits," Johnny said.

"Why didn't you use the faucet!"

"We were tryin' to save time," I replied.

"Save time! Everbody's been done for ten minutes and lookin' for you! And you're soakin' wet!"

Johnny said, "Our mess kits fell in the creek and—"

"Spare us the explanation! Just get outa there and let's go!"

"Yes sir," we said. We gathered our shoes and socks, scrambled up the bank, and followed the dads. We could hear them muttering: "Jesus H. Christ, I had a... Easy, Sam, they're just... Same two every fuckin'... Well, boys'll be... A coupla airheads is..."

When we got to the campground the dads had to decide who would take Johnny and me back to Tulsa. One reluctantly volunteered to. Another reluctantly offered to keep him company. As all the rest got in the other cars and drove away, we threw our gear into the trunk of the volunteer's car and started to get in the back seat when he said that he didn't want our wet smelly clothes in his car, so we were going to have to walk ourselves dry.

Johnny and I knew that making us walk was a punishment as well as a method for drying out, but we didn't care. We walked along the rocky road leading from the campground to the highway for two or three miles as the two dads followed us at idle speed, their faces sullen and glowering, whereas Johnny and I were having a good ole time. We talked about all the trouble we had been in, stretching truth into lies and lies into legends. We punched each other in the shoulder to see who could take the most pain, tried to hip each other off the road, kicked rocks like footballs to see who had the better leg, threw rocks to see who had the stronger arm, threw rocks at signs and birds to see who had the better aim. We turned the punishment into pleasure, which probably pissed the dads off even more.

When we were finally dry they let us in the car. We fell asleep and didn't wake up until they let me off at my house, then drove off with Johnny, too late for a round of golf, I'm sure.

After greetings with Mom and Chris, plus the story of

what had happened, I went into the bathroom to take a pee and discovered something amazing and alarming: a tick, its head buried in the head of my penis. I felt too old to ask Mom for her help in this predicament—I was in the thick of puberty—so I fetched my Scout's Manual to see what to do. It said I should not, absolutely not, pull the tick out. Its head would remain embedded and cause an infection. No, I was to burn it. The pain would make the tick back out of its host, the book said, but I imagined the match flame burning the shit out of the host, this organ that had a future I was beginning to anticipate. I read on: it said sticking a heated pin into the tick's body should do the trick. That seemed relatively safe, so I tried it, several times. The tick obviously hadn't read the Manual: it didn't budge. But I couldn't just leave it there, because if I did my poor ole dick would get infected, turn all black and sprout puss-filled sores, then rot off at the stem. I decided to take my chances, yanked the tick out, flushed it down the toilet, and years later engendered some kids. So much for the Scout's Manual.

About a year and a half after Johnny and I joined Troop 37, Curly Fowler quit and a man named Seager took over. His son Danny was a real nice kid, loose and easy-going, and a very good athlete, but Mr. Seager was uptight, nervous, controlling, always afraid of what we might do. So, like a good Scoutmaster, he organized activities that would help us earn merit badges. But when you're used to being on your own, organized activities just don't cut it, and many of us, including Johnny and me, couldn't have cared less about merit badges. The tension between his efforts to control us and our efforts to resist—we would sneak off, day and night—drove him dotty, so he took us camping less and less often. And when we did go, he watched us more and more closely, allowing us to do less and less on our own, so we disobeyed more and more and he got more and more uptight and controlling, so we... it was a vicious cycle, the upshot of which was, we had less and less fun.

One night we were acting way too wild for Mr. Seager's comfort. We had made the bonfire too big, we were recklessly leaping across it and wrestling too near it, we were whipping and poking each other with the marshmallow and hotdog sticks—we were endangering life and limb, threatening the forest with fire!—so he ordered us to put out the fire and turn in, even though it was a good hour too early to be turning in.

When we got the fire out it was close to pitch black. Just a sliver of moon, a pale hint of moonlight. Richard Hudson discovered he had forgotten to bring his sleeping bag. Johnny was still messing around with the embers of the bonfire, so Richard slipped into his.

"C'mon, Richard," I said, "you can't do that. It's Johnny's."

"Tough shit," Richard said, zipping it up. "It's mine now."

"It's not yours," someone said, and another added, "Go see Mr. Seager. He can probably fix you up with some blankets or sumpn."

"Why should I? I'm fixed up already."

Then we heard Johnny. "Hey! Who's in my sleeping bag?"

Richard was quietly giggling, so I said, "Richard."

Johnny asked, "Why don't you sleep in your own bag, Richard?"

"I am," Richard said. "Finder's keeper's."

"Finder's keeper's my ass. It's my bag, Richard. Now get out of it."

"Make me," Richard said, who happened to be considerably bigger and stronger than the rest of us.

"Okay. If you don't get out by the count of three, I'm gonna piss on your head."

"Oh, scare me why dontcha?"

"One."

"Piss on me, you piss on your own sleepin' bag."

"Two."

"You can't even see where to pee," Richard scoffed.

"No, but I can hear, dumbsmack. Three."

We could hear pee squirting and splashing, then Richard bellowing, "Oh my Gawd! It's in my eyes! Oh Jesus!" and then we could hear him bawling and crawling out of the sleeping bag and running to the dads' big tent, yelling, "Mr. Seager! Mr. Seager!"

We were laughing and congratulating Johnny when we heard footsteps approaching, then saw a flashlight beam dart around until it landed on Johnny's face. "Why'd you urinate on Richard's face, Nilson?"

"He stole my sleeping bag."

"It's my bag!" Richard cried.

Johnny hollered, "Bullshit, you lyin' sonofabitch!"

"Urinating on a fellow scout right in his face, and now cussing like a sailor—you're sleeping in one of the cars tonight, Nilson!"

"But it's Johnny's bag!" we yelled.

"There's no excuse for that kind of behavior! So get on out of here, Nilson!"

"I'll go with you, Johnny," I said.

"Get back down, Duncan! He's not fit to sleep with anyone else!" Mr. Seager stood there, a large shadow looming over us. Johnny started walking toward the parking area and Mr. Seager said, "Sorry for the mishap, Richard. I'll get you some blankets," and he walked away.

When he was out of earshot we turned on Richard. "Lyin' sonofabitch! Rat! Chickenshit!" The rest of the guys picked up their sleeping bags and moved away. I picked up mine and carried it to the parking area. I went from car to car until I found Johnny in a backseat. I got in beside him and spread my bag over the two of us.

"That's it," Johnny said.

"That's it," I agreed.

"Fuckin' asshole," he added.

"Both of 'em," I said. In silence we contemplated Richard's skullduggery and Mr. Seager's numbskullery for a

30  *Low Crimes and Misdemeanors*

bit, then I started laughing and said, "But pissin' in Richard's face was great, man!"

Johnny laughed and said, "And he can have the damn sleepin' bag, if it means so much to him." We talked some more about the sad state scouting had come to, and finally fell asleep.

And that was it, our farewell to Troop 37.


## *Hope Lumber*

One day a guy named Donald Jones asked if I'd like to play in the yard of Hope Lumber after school. I wasn't sure what playing in a lumberyard meant, but I said sure. It was only two blocks away, on East Eleventh Street, better known as Route or Highway 66, the main thoroughfare of my youth. We climbed over the chain link fence with the three strands of barbed wire on top, then ran around on the stacks of lumber. The thing that made it fun was that the lumber was stacked not only high—fifteen, twenty feet—but also at uneven heights, so we weren't just running, we were jumping from one stack to another, now up, now down, as if we were leaping from building to building in a movie chase. When some workers saw us they made the fun even funner by having a fit, screaming at us to get off the lumber for God's sake, it could fall on us, get the hell out before we got hurt—the common sort of grownup hysteria we thought was hilarious. A few days later we did it again, with the same result: a great time eventually destroyed by nervous nellies. After a while we couldn't even get over the fence before being caught.

Other than the lumberyard Donald and I didn't have much in common. I spent the night with him once. The next morning we went to his folks' church. It was a large Baptist church, and while they went to the service, Donald and I went to his Sunday School class. The teacher, a big man in a very nice suit, spent the entire hour quietly lecturing us on niggers, commies, and catholics, all of them decidedly lower-case but dire threats nonetheless. All three were trying to take over the country, and we had to resist them by every means possible. At collection time he dropped into the plate a fifty dollar bill, the equivalent of at least three hundred bucks today. Perhaps he was trying to demonstrate the virtue of generosity, but I thought he was showing off.

I never went back to that church, and I never played with Donald again.


### High Times at Highland

Johnny played golf, not regularly, like his dad, but occasionally, probably because none of his buddies played, including me. We couldn't afford it. But one day, when we were twelve or so, he wanted me to play a round with him, offering to pay my bus fare and my green fees, and he would buy me all the food and drink I wanted, and he would even carry my bag the whole round himself—when Johnny wanted something, he had to have it, and he begged and bugged and badgered me until I finally gave in. We took the bus to the nearest public course, Highland Golf Club at Twenty-First and Yale. It was hot, and Johnny had some extra money to burn (Johnny always had some extra money to burn), and he didn't want to carry his own clubs, much less mine, so he rented an electric cart, a new convenience at the time. We played three or four holes, got bored looking for my errant balls, then got a great idea: to play with the cart.

The game we devised was simple. One of us would drive and try to throw the other, who couldn't hold on to anything, off the cart. When the other got thrown, he became the driver. We whipped the cart back and forth, started and stopped as herkily-jerkily as possible, accelerated then slammed on the brakes or made a ninety degree turn, or both. Soon we were not only throwing each other out of the cart, we were rolling the cart over as well— both passenger and driver leaping out to avoid getting smashed. Which wasn't easy—avoiding injury—because we were laughing so hard.

We played golf-cart derby until the battery went dead, a good two hours.

Once in a while we went back to Highland and actually played a round of golf. When we found balls that others had lost, we kept them, naturally: finders-keepers, the law of the jungle. After playing, we walked to the bus stop along the barbed wire fence that bordered the course and usually found a few more. One day on our way to the bus stop, we passed a red-faced foursome swishing their clubs around in the rough near the fence. Then Johnny stopped and said to me, "Holy shit, Jay, they're looking for a ball."

I said, "Damn, John, you're right. And we've got a bunch."

We walked back to the foursome, sold them some balls, and we were in business. Every several days we went out to Highland and combed the roadside along the fence, then sold our find to golfers passing by. Soon we started climbing through the fence onto the course, not only to search for balls, but to wash the ones we'd found and sell them at the nearest tee.

We got even bolder. We started hanging out in this ravine that separated the tee from the green of a par three hole. It was a lovely spot, with a little stream slipping through, and bushes clumped here and there, and tall sycamores providing shade, and we always found some balls we could wash right in the stream. Every once in a while we'd hear a ball smack into a tree. We'd find it, stomp it into the mud and stand there. Pretty soon a golfer or two would walk down into the ravine, looking. When they saw us they'd ask, "Yall see a ball come down here?"

"No sir," one of us would say, and the other would add something like, "We heard it, but we haven't been able to find it."

And they would cuss, look around a bit more, then

leave. We would dig the ball out of the mud, wash it off, and add it to our stash.

Just about the time we felt like we pretty well owned Highland, we were lounging in the ravine one afternoon enjoying our demesne when we heard a tractor approaching. It quickly got louder and louder, until all of a sudden it appeared at the top of the ridge. Behind the wheel was a man wearing a white T-shirt, a baseball cap, and a grim determined look. He didn't pause a second, just came tearing down the hill straight at us. Johnny and I took off running uphill the other way. The driver didn't slow down, so we had to run for our lives, it felt like, as he drove the tractor through the stream and up the hill, gaining on us. We got clear of the trees and saw the street on the other side of a field and some ten yards or so of thick bushes. We sprinted across the field, hearing the tractor gaining on us, and got to the bushes just as it was about to run us over.

To our dismay, the bushes turned out to be raspberries, which we literally tore through, thousands of sharp little thorns tearing clothes and skin, until we got to the barbed wire fence. Hurriedly stooping through, we tore some more cloth and skin. We looked back and saw that the driver had stopped at the bushes. He shot us the finger, his sign of victory. We shot him the finger back, our gesture of defiance. But also of surrender, truth to tell, for we knew we were out of business.

But it had been good while it lasted.


### *The Lothario of East Fourth Place*

He was three or four years older than me, a wiry little guy, the only child of a wiry little couple named Barr who lived three houses down and across the street. I never knew his parents' first names. They kept to themselves. Upon seeing me they'd sometimes say "Hi," but never "How are you?" or "How's your mom?" or anything like that. Usually

34         *Low Crimes and Misdemeanors*

they said nothing at all. Mr. Barr had a natty mustache and thick wavy hair that he kept immaculately combed. Mrs. Barr wore her hair short and frosted. They both wore their jeans tight. Except to go somewhere outside the neighbor-hood, they never came outside, not even to tend their yard. Their boy Doug did that.

Doug didn't hang around with the guys on the street much. He'd chat with us now and then, but he didn't shoot baskets, didn't play any kind of ball, didn't go into any-body's house, never had anybody in his house. At the age of thirteen or so he started caddying at the Tulsa Country Club and took up golf, but so far as I could tell from our occa-sional conversations, he played by himself. He had a smug, tough-guy smirk on his face, as if he always knew a lot of things we didn't but would like to, and yet I instinctively doubted him. I doubted because Doug radiated sleaze like a nimbus. Not slick-sleazy, like certain salesmen and preach-ers, but crass-sleazy, like barkers at strip-joints and carnies.

But perhaps it was that very sleaze that served him so well in the one area where he really did know a lot, where he was the envy of all the neighborhood boys: the area of girls. Doug always had a girlfriend, his girlfriends always had pretty faces along with terrific boobs and legs and butts, and he could prove it, with the dozens and dozens of photos he took of them in their homes while their parents were gone. The girls were always in various degrees of undress and in every pinup pose imaginable on beds, on couches, on tables, on counter tops, on stairs, on ladders, as well as in chairs, in bathtubs, in showers, in kitchen sinks even. He knew just where to draw the line to get his photos developed (these were the days just before Polaroid), how much exposure he could get away with, how much boob and buttock and crotch. He always carried a wad of these photos around, and he delighted in showing them to us, offering his expert opinion on this angle or that, this pose or that, this feature or that.

We knew that he really did take them himself and

that the "subjects" really were his girlfriends, because one after another he brought these girls to Fourth Place and in broad daylight would neck with them in the alley right on the unfenced property line of the Amstutz's back yard, of all places, of all people. Why there? Maybe as a ribald rebuke of their straight-laced, tee-totaling, Southern Baptist piety. Rumor had it that Mr. Amstutz called Doug's folks once to complain, that Mrs. Barr asked if Doug and his sweet thing had their clothes on, that Mr. Amstutz said yes, and that Mrs. Barr told him not to bother her unless they had taken them off.

Actually, the word "neck" doesn't do Doug and his sweeties, or the Amstutzes, justice. No word or phrase does. Bill and coo? Pet? Make out? Not even close. Because what they did was, they locked their mouths in a wide-open uvula-deep French kiss while taking turns lying on top of each other, massaging boobs and butt and crotch, wrapping legs and bumping privates, and they carried on like this for so long they became just another feature of the alley's landscape, along with the bushes, the telephone poles, the fences, the trash cans, the ruts in the lane. So the Amstutzes weren't just being prudes, albeit they were certainly prudish. Because I submit that even swingers in this post-Puritan, anything-goes age of ours would have issues with a couple of teenagers dry-fucking in broad daylight right on their property line.

We boys wondered how Doug met these girls. How he talked them into letting him take dirty pictures of them. How he got them to make out like that, even in private, much less in public. And, of course, whether he actually screwed them, and what was that like, 'cause we were dyin', dyin' to know. We also wondered what the girls saw in him that was so attractive. What they saw in him that they didn't see in guys like us. But we never found out because we wouldn't give him the satisfaction of asking.

He must have had some mighty fragrant pheromones. And he certainly had a genius. But so far as I know, he never turned it to professional account. Never became a pimp or a pornographer. The last time I saw him, he was maybe twenty-two working full-time in the produce section of a supermarket—i.e., handling vegetables and fruit, which, however erotic in a subliminal, Freudian sort of way, was a far cry from photographing and handling the tootsies of his teenage years.

Did Doug miss his calling? Betray his gifts? Or did he channel his id into monogamy? Or get saved? The moral of his story eludes me. But the memories of his photos and his romps in the alley don't elude me at all. On the contrary....

### Winter Sports

We got more snow and sleet in Oklahoma than most Northerners realize. Sometimes it got cold enough to ice skate on ponds in the parks. Cold enough long enough even to play ice hockey, a game we made even more violent by virtue of our ineptitude on skates. Most of the time, though, the temperature hovered between thirty and forty. Precipitation usually fell in the form of sleet or wet soggy snow. But sleet and wet soggy snow had their advantages: sleet for sledding because it was faster and wilder than snow, and soggy snow for snowmen and, better yet—far better yet—for snowballs.

At school and in our neighborhood we had fine, fierce snowball fights, as kids do wherever there is snow. But besides hurling snowballs at each other, we hurled them at cars and busses and trucks, something I haven't seen kids do since I left Oklahoma over fifty years ago. And I don't understand it, because plastering a moving vehicle, especially the windshield of a moving vehicle, the snowball splattering on impact like paint fired from a gun...well, all I can say is, the kids who don't do that don't know the fun they're missing.

Or the excitement. Many drivers—those still in touch

with their inner child—enjoyed the sport as much as we did. But not all. If they spotted us before we fired, some would stop and describe to us the dangers we posed to motorists: a snowball hitting the windshield, the startled and temporarily blinded driver smashing into another vehicle or a tree or a pedestrian, the injuries, the hospital, the death, the funeral, the grieving friends and family. We would listen and pretend to agree. Others would tell us that if we threw at their car, they would call the police. Still others said they would chase us down and beat the living shit out of us. Whatever they said, when they began driving away we let 'em have it.

One guy I particularly remember. Not seeing that Johnny and I were about to get him good, he stopped, got out, and walked toward us holding up a photo of a Beagle and asking, "Have you boys seen this dog? She got loose a couple of hours ago and my kids are crazy with worry." We looked at the photo and said no we hadn't. He asked, "Would yall mind keeping an eye out for her?" We said sure. He gave us a card. "If yall do see her, her name is Suzy. She'll mind. She's real gentle. Just take her and give me a call at this number, okay?" We said sure. "Thanks, fellas. I really appreciate it." We said no problem, be our pleasure.

Then he got back in his car, took off, and we plastered him. He slammed on his brakes sliding to a stop and leaping out of the car screaming, "You no-good sonsobitches!" He ran at us in a frenzy, slipping and sliding in his street shoes, scooping up snow and packing it with his bare hands and hurling the snowballs at us along with furious volleys of profanity—"Fuckin' assholes! Treacherous goddamn rats! Rotten cocksuckin' little weasels!" Darting this way and that to duck the snowballs and stay out of his reach, we could hardly keep our feet we were laughing so hard. Which of course made him all the madder, all the funnier.

He finally gave up and returned to his car, which was idling in the middle of the street, the driver's door open. We said, "We'll call you if we find your dog."

"Fuck you, you shits!" he hollered, and drove off.

The irony was—and this was one reason we found his fury so funny—if we saw Suzy, we *would* have taken her in and called him up. We didn't want his kids to lose their pet. But we didn't see why we shouldn't wallop his car with snowballs. As we said after he drove off, the poor guy was mixing apples and oranges.


## *Class Politics*

In elementary school I always got good grades for academics and bad grades for "deportment," according to the lingo of the day. I was a cut-up, a clown, a loudmouth, a pain in the ass. When I moved on and up to Woodrow Wilson Junior High I didn't see any reason to change my ways—*I* was having fun—so I didn't.

In seventh-grade music, though, I went above and beyond my usual misbehavior, because I heartily disliked the teacher. Her name I don't remember—I'll call her Ms. Melody—but her I do: a middle-aged, chunky, solicitous woman with short-cropped gray hair and no sense of play or humor or, as far as I was concerned, taste. I couldn't stand the songs she had us sing, so I'd sing them loudly and off-key. Also, in a whisper slathered with sarcasm, I'd share my opinions of her and her music with my classmates. She would gesture to me to stop, and I would stop, briefly, then I'd resume my running commentary. One time she walked over to me, put her arm around my shoulder, and asked so all could hear, "Don't you like this class, Jeffrey?" I said no. "Don't you like music?" I said no. And then, her earnest, solicitous face right in mine, "Don't you like me?" I said no.

Ms. Melody banished me to a corner in the back of the room and forbid me to sing for the rest of the year. Which was fine by me, partly because it seemed fair enough, given the degree of my insolence, but also because I didn't want to sing the sorry songs she selected anyway, and I could while away the period reading. But then, come the third quarter, I had a major brainstorm.

First some background information. Ms. Melody structured her class as if it was a democracy. We had elections at the beginning of each quarter, so that we could change "officers" every nine weeks, thereby giving more students a chance to experience the privileges and burdens of political office. There were three officers: president, vice-president, and secretary. (Treasurer would have been too obviously *de trop*, since there was no budget.) The president called the class to order and the secretary read the minutes. The president asked if there was any old or new business. The only business we had was the songs we'd been working on, which had already been covered in the minutes, and the songs we were going to work on, so we dispatched the old and the new business in short order, then got to work singing her lame-ass songs. All the vice-president did was stand by in case the president had a heart attack or got assassinated or something.

Well, when election time came for the third quarter, I nominated myself for president and, to Ms. Melody's chagrin, I won hands down. Oh, it was sweet, let me tell you—sweet!—to see her trapped in her own silly structure. Because what could she do? Nullify the election? Then there wouldn't even be the pretense of a democracy. So she had to eat the results, to accept the fact that the class not only enjoyed my antics, but obviously shared at least some of my sentiments as well. And I got the pleasure of being pariah and president, outlaw and officer, at the same time.

But the price I paid for my misbehavior was greater than any I'd paid before: Ms. Melody not only prophesied that I would wind up in the state pen, she flunked me. My first (but not my last) F.

### Mindlessness in Math

At the beginning of eighth-grade math class one day, the teacher, Mr. Hargis—a short, pot-bellied, near-sighted, nasal-voiced man with an accent straight off the farm—came to me and demanded, "Looky here, Duncan: did you do that?" Following his finger, I looked down. There, scratched clear across the desk top in large, crude, cursive script, was my name and then some: Jeffff.

"That?" I asked, pointing in turn, as if he could have had something else in mind.

"Yes, that!"

Then I remembered: the day before, in the warm, drowsy spring afternoon, while Hargis was droning on about whatever and I, in my customary state of intellectual stupor and glandular riot, was as usual slumped in my seat rubbing my knees against the ass of the girl sitting in front of me, blonde sexy Laura LaRue—even her name was sexy, the Frenchiness of it, the tonguey alliteration—and as I was wondering if she was enjoying the feel I was copping as much as I was, if in fact she was even aware I was rubbing her buns because she never seemed to be, but then how could she not be, and after all, she could slump and scooch her butt out of my knees' reach but never did—amidst all this knee-jerk, erotic reverie, I was doodling my pencil on the desk top and discovered it had a snag in the tip which cut right through the veneer, and so, while consciously getting hot and bothered kneeing Laura's buttocks, I absent-mindedly scratched my name clear across the top. But I saw no reason to admit it. "No, I didn't," I said.

Mr. Hargis handed me one of my quizzes and pointed to my name at the top, then at the desk, then back at the quiz. "So how do you explain your handwriting on your desk?"

"Someone musta forged my name."

"Looky here, Duncan, either you admit it and we take care o' this matter between ourselves, or I take you to Mr. Tharp and you'll be in trouble sure 'nough. What's it gonna be?"

Mr. Tharp was the vice-principal, a thirty-five-ish soft-spoken man who wore the whitest shirts I'd ever seen and who looked like he had once played professional football—he was that big. No one wanted to mess with him. "How do you want us to take care of it?"

"For you to refinish the desk."

"That's all?"

"That's all."

"You got a deal," I said. I carried the desk down to wood shop where every day I worked on it for an hour before school and for an hour after, scraping and sanding it by hand since there were no power tools, and taking out all the other names and initials that had been carved and gouged in it through the years, and sanding and varnishing and steel-wooling and varnishing until I finally got the desk-top looking like new.

Had I been cast in a different mold, cut from a different bolt, endowed with a different genetic combo, this punishment might have proved a paradoxical and providential turning point in my life, leading to a career in high-end woodworking of some sort or other—making custom furniture, say, or building yachts—but it didn't. I am what I am and therefore it was what it was, an exercise in boredom that lasted, not for *just* a month, but for a *whole* month.


### *Paying the Price*

Sometimes I misbehaved even in classes I liked. Gym, for instance. Our routine was to suit up in the locker room, then run a lap clockwise around the block (half a mile), then do whatever was on the agenda for the day: soccer, flag football, basketball, track and field. One morning, thinking it would be cute to cheat, I talked a classmate, Bobby Joe Roberts, into cheating with me. The coaches didn't leave the locker room with us, so, I reasoned, they wouldn't see what we did. Instead of turning right on the sidewalk and running with our classmates around the block, we turned left and sprinted down the sloping sidewalk a half-block to the corner, which was the last turn and which had a berm three or four feet high. There we crouched until our classmates came along, then we joined them, huffing and puffing as if we had run the entire distance. After a minute or two pretending to get our breath, we sat down with our classmates to get our instructions for the day.

Coach Downs, a potbellied redhead, took a stance in front of us and said, "Boys, two of you took a shortcut today, and we don't believe in takin' shortcuts. Now, if those two fellas fess up, all that'll happen is they'll take two laps insteada one and that'll be the end o' the matter."

Bobby Joe nudged me. Even though I realized I had reasoned wrong, I frowned back and whispered, "He's bluffin'."

"Okay, let's make this easy. One of you has the initials BJ, and the other's a red-head. If you two guys get up and take a couple o' laps we'll be quits; if you don't, well... What'll it be?"

Bobby Joe whispered, "Let's run."

"Go ahead, if that's what you wanta do," I whispered. "But I'm stickin' it out."

Bobby Joe didn't stand up. Coach Downs said, "Okay, Roberts, Duncan, if you wanta be stupid, that's your choice. Come here." We went to the place he indicated. "Now the rest of you line up in two rows about four feet apart with about three feet between the rows." Buzzing with curiosity and excitement, the fifty or so boys lined up as Coach Downs had directed. "Good," he said. "Now boys, we're gonna have a gauntlet. What that means is, Roberts, you first, then you, Duncan, run down the middle between the two lines. And boys, as they're passin' by, let 'em have it. Hit 'em, slap 'em, elbow 'em, kick 'em, whatever you like, just as long as you do it *hard*. Yall got that?"

"Yeah!" they hollered. "You bet, coach! Got it!" Not that they were pissed off at Bobby Joe and me for cheating—

there was nothing wrong with that—but that they were hopped up about having license to knock the crap out of a couple of the bigger, better athletes in the class. Which is what they did: knock the crap out of us as we smashed our way through their swinging feet, legs, hands, elbows, fists.

Okay, I'll admit it: I liked running that gauntlet. It bore out the image of myself that I favored: tough guy with bruises, cuts, abrasions. But the usual punishments?—staying after school, writing a sentence hundreds of times? I hated them, they were so boring, mindless. Yet I wouldn't stop doing the things that provoked them—eating candy and chewing gum in class (big no-no's back then), blowing paper wads through a straw, shooting paper-clips with rubber bands, whispering to fellow students, offering unsolicited smart-ass observations to the teacher and the class at large. The punishments were the price for misbehaving, and I was willing to pay: the misbehavior was more satisfying than the price was painful. As for the grades, the frequent C's and D's and the occasional F that I got for the next six years and that drove Mom into a dither, I really didn't give a damn.

### *Appropriate Measures*

One of our haunts on the T.U. campus was Harwell Gym, next to Kendall Hall. It was an old-school gym. The basketball court was on the second floor. Above the court and surrounding it was a running track that cut across the corners of the court, making corner shots impossible. We liked to race around the track: leaning into the steeply banked turns at each end gave us an exaggerated sense of speed. We also liked to play basketball there—a full-length court with a wood floor beat the hell out of hoops nailed over garage doors.

I spent many hours in that gym. It was maybe a five-minute trot from the house, and it was often open and unoccupied. Sometimes I went alone, sometimes with

44 *Low Crimes and Misdemeanors*

buddies. The team I played for in junior high practiced there. It got to the point that I considered it my gym, just as I regarded the practice fields on campus as my fields, and the campus itself as my campus. To the point that one winter Sunday afternoon, when I was thirteen or so, Johnny and I, finding that the doors were locked, circled the building trying the huge double-hung windows, found one unlocked, managed to open it (it was so heavy it took both of us to push it up), and crawled in. I knew we were breaking a rule or two, but I didn't feel it was wrong: rather, it felt as if I'd been locked out of my own house and I was taking appropriate measures to get in. We had been playing for thirty minutes or so when two cops barged in hollering, "How'd yall git in here?"

"We walked in," I said, feeling like it was none of their business.

"You walked in? Haw! The doors're locked!"

"We walked in through a winda," Johnny offered.

"You snuck in through a winda, you mean! What for?"

"To play basketball," I said.

"I bet to play basketball. Yall're lookin' for sumpn to swipe."

"We just came to play basketball!" I said: "Honest!"

"Play my ass."

"If we wanted to steal sumpn," Johnny noted, "why would we hang around to git caught?"

"Cause yall're dumbass kids, that's why. C'mon. We're takin' ya to the station."

"But we haven't stolen anything!" I protested.

"C'mon, we said: move it!"

"For what?" Johnny asked. "Playin' basketball?"

"For breakin' and enterin'."

They shepherded us down the stairs and into the backseat of their patrol car. On the way downtown the cop in the passenger seat, a heavy-breathing fat-faced hick, kept saying, "Didn't your folks learn you boys no better'n that?

You cain't just break into places cause you feel like it. That's a crime. I cain't believe your folks didn't learn yall no better'n that." Along the way we passed a few guys we knew. We waved. Looking startled, then amused, some waved back, others pointed and laughed, still others laughed and shot us the finger, and we responded to them all in kind.

We got to the station and nothing much happened. Some more lecture on breaking and entering, then on juvenile delinquency and reform school, a little addendum about how they were going to let us off the hook this time, but we better not ever pull a stunt like that again or they'd throw the book at us, then they told us to call our parents. Mom didn't have a car, so we called Johnny's. They told us to take the bus.

Our parents didn't punish us. Breaking and entering? We just wanted to play basketball.


### *Throwing Papers*

Johnny and I both got jobs delivering the *Tulsa World*, the morning newspaper. We had to have morning routes so we could do our sports in the afternoon. Our routes were side-by-side, so we picked up our papers at the same place, the Crown Texaco station at the corner of Fifteenth and Lewis. While we folded our papers in the early-morning dark, we talked about sports, friends, parents, school, girls. We talked about girls a lot. The scope of our interest was pretty limited, though—we usually focused on tits, and even more particularly on authenticity, trying to determine who wore falsies and who had the real deals.

Our routes were lucrative—we each made around sixty, sixty-five dollars a month, at a time when a movie cost a kid a dime, an adult a quarter, and tuition at the University of Oklahoma was three bucks an hour.

But when is enough ever enough? Johnny and I decided we wanted to put more money in our purses, and we figured out a way to do it, by ordering our Sunday delivery a dozen copies short, then stealing the difference from the news rack in front of the not-yet-open drugstore catty-corner from the gas station. Those were one hundred percent profit. Until one Sunday when, as we were transferring the papers from the rack to our bags, a pickup truck roared around the corner and screeched to a stop. A man jumped out and hollered, "So you're the sonsobitches been stealin' my papers!" Johnny and I stopped.

"We came up short," Johnny explained as the man counted the papers in the rack.

"Two dozen copies!"

"We came up real short," I said.

"Yall've been comin' up real short for five straight Sundays, goddamnit! Why don'tcha order the number you need!"

"We're lousy at math?" I offered.

"Don't give me that shit."

"We're just tryin' to augment our income," Johnny said.

"Well, augment your fuckin' income at someone else's expense!" he bellowed. "Now put the papers back, and don't ever pull that stunt again or I'll git your unaugmented asses fired! After I kick 'em first! You got that?"

"We need them for our customers," I pointed out.

"Then pay me," he said.

Having no choice, we paid him. He got back into his pickup and peeled off.

"Well, you win some, you lose some," Johnny philosophized.

"Hey," I suddenly realized, "he didn't make us pay for the other papers we swiped."

"You lose some, you win some," Johnny said.

Then I said, "Hey, John—where in hell'd you get that 'augment our income' bit?"

"My dad. He's always talkin' about augmenting his income. You know, make it bigger."

"Oh," I said. "Well I'd like to augment my dick."

"Now you're talkin'," Johnny said. "Dick is more important than income any day."

Having our priorities in order, we didn't raid any more racks. We figured the man in the pickup would have told everyone to be on the lookout.

### Sosh

Toward the end of the summer after seventh grade Johnny invited me to a party at his house. Now I had spent plenty of time at Johnny's house—we often spent entire weekends with each other—but he'd never had a party. He said he'd been going to these parties that summer, and they were really neat, with girls there as well as guys, and they slow-danced to forty-fives, and the girls were really neat, real pretty and fun, and there was pop and snacks, and everyone talked and had a really neat time. For a guy who could come up with "augment our income," Johnny was remarkably inarticulate about these parties, but what he lacked in words he made up for in fervor. They were really neat, and he was going to have one, and he wanted me to come, and he had a girl lined up for me name of Judy who was really cute and fun, and I was to wear a nice sport shirt and slacks—no jeans!—and to be sure and shine my shoes and comb my hair.

I hadn't realized the social implications of puberty yet—of any implications beyond random spontaneous hard-ons and nocturnal emissions, plus taking hands-on measures to humor my fits of lust—so I was wondering what in God's name had come over John. Slacks? Shine my shoes and comb my hair? And who'd been having these strange parties that I'd never heard about? What was going on anyway!?

Well, Johnny was my best friend, and he was a boat load of fun, and when he had fun I had fun, so I said okay, sure, thanks, sounds great. And damn if he didn't give me some more instructions on grooming and etiquette, as if I came from some country that didn't use furniture or toothbrushes yet. So I went to the party all spiffed up and on my best behavior, and this girl Judy was okay, kinda cute but quiet, and the party was just like John had said: there were six or seven couples, and Kenny Teel and Danny Porter were there—other buddies I played sports and hung around with—and we slow-danced to forty-fives, and drank pop and ate sandwiches and chips and made small talk, and us guys horsed around a little, smacking each others' shoulders, elbowing each other in the gut, hipping each other in mid-dance, but not much else, certainly no belching or farting or goosing each other, not with the girls there. And then it was over.

A little later, after Johnny and I had gone to bed—for I spent the night—he said, "Wasn't that the best time, Jay? Wasn't it just great?"

And I said, "Yeah, John: great."

"Wasn't it just the best time you ever had?"

And I said, "The best, man: the best."

In truth, though, I had actually found it pretty boring. But I knew that it marked an end and a beginning, though what it was beginning I didn't know, only that it was major, and that I was supposed to have had the time of my life, so I persuaded myself that I had. Not altogether, however, because I remember wondering how Johnny had found the party to be that much fun, and if Kenny and Danny felt the same as he did, and if so, what was I missing?

Johnny's party turned out to be my informal inaugural ball. I became what was known as a sosh, a word that rhymes with *gauche*, and that, like Quaker, was a term of contempt or praise depending on who said it and how. Being a sosh meant being in the in-crowd, the kids that the out-crowd envied or scorned or both. It meant going to many parties like Johnny's, plus larger parties at public rental places—Braden Hall in town, Robinwood out south of town—plus an occasional formal at the T.U. student union, where the guys wore suits (tuxes came later, in high school) and the girls, after getting their hair done at a beauty salon and their faces done at Merle Norman, wore formal dresses that the guys bedecked with a corsage: carnations from those of us in pinched circumstances, roses or orchids from guys of greater means.

By the end of that summer I had learned that to be really in, I should take ballroom lessons at a place called Skilly's in Utica Square. Utica Square was a new and very chichi shopping mall across from St. John's Hospital at Twenty-First and Utica, and Skilly's, everyone said, was the place to take dance lessons. Johnny signed up with me.

The Skillys, a middle-aged snip-snap couple always decked out to the nines—he in a suit with a handkerchief in the breast pocket that matched his tie, she in a glitzy cocktail dress and high heels—started with ballroom etiquette: how a guy should ask a girl to dance, how a girl should respond yes or no, how a guy should escort the girl onto the dance floor, how he should take her right hand in his left and place his right hand on the small of her back, etc. Then they taught the dances themselves, and they taught them exactly so: foxtrot, swing, waltz, cha-cha-cha, and I don't remember what else because Johnny and I quickly found all this prissy fuss-and-bother to be excruciating. Even worse, all the good-looking girls of the in-crowd had gone to Skilly's the year before, so we were left with the scraps, the remains, the dogs, as we variously put it, finding no expression too brutal.

One evening I wound up with a thick-waisted, heavy-footed girl with hamburger breath and no rhythm who I had to push around like a refrigerator, and I decided then and there that if I didn't learn the correct way to foxtrot, I could fake it. And if I couldn't fake it, fuck it: I was done with this shit, period. After class I found that Johnny had come to the same conclusion. We only wondered what had taken us so long.

Being a sosh meant you had to go steady. Had to. So I found a girl who was unattached—a nice girl named Sarah

Rudolph who I found mildly attractive—and, according to protocol, I dug up a ring that she wore on a chain around her neck. We talked every night until our parents pried the phones from our ears, and we met at movies, and we went to parties that Mom drove us to and from, and sometimes double-dated with some other guy's folk doing the driving, and we slow-danced and kissed and even went so far as to French kiss, and then, for some reason I can't recollect, I broke up with her.

I went steady next with Mary Montgomery. Mary reminded me some of Grace Kelly—tall, slender, blonde, clever, cool and playful at the same time. I found her quite attractive. But, to add some variety to the usual pattern of phone-talk, movies, and parties, we played tennis once, and it was so tedious dinking the ball back and forth and fetching her hits that had gone astray, which she found amusing, that soon thereafter I broke up with her. That's not much of a reason to break up with a girl, I realize, but then I didn't need much: even as teenagers go, I wasn't very deep.

My next steady was Debbie Morgan. She was the opposite of Mary: short, brunette, bright and perky. I found her very attractive, and she liked me too. Her parents, on the other hand, considered me bad news. From days of yore at Carter Oil, her dad knew my dad and declared, in accord with Old Testament genetics, that no son of Bob Duncan's could be anything but a bad apple and ruled me off limits for his daughter, and thus, price being a function of scarcity, he doubled our value in each other's eyes. We went underground, going steady on the sly, with our friends conspiring to help us as covers and go-betweens. It was heady stuff, far more interesting and satisfying than my previous romances, but even so, by the time I was wrapping up junior high, I was burned out on sosh life. Living the straight, year-book life of adolescence—going steady, going to movies and malt shops, going to dances and parties, yakking for hours on the phone about anything that came to mind and nothing much—it all took way too much time and attention when there were far more exciting and fun things to do, things with buddies.

And wouldn't you know it? Johnny had come to the exact same conclusion.


## *On the Town*

At Wilson Johnny and I had gotten to know a couple of guys we liked a lot: Jack Walcott and Rollen Chesser. In our eyes they came from good families. Jack's older brother Ben was a state champion wrestler, and Rolly's older brother Ralph was an all-conference halfback at Will Rogers High School, playing alongside my neighborhood hero who was also all-conference, Don Brooks. Jack was short, fat, and baby-faced, with a peaches-and-cream complexion, a big sweet smile, and big deep dimples. He was a master of useless skills: he could punch a light bag with the finesse of a professional boxer; he won championships yo-yoing; he played a mean game of snooker; and he could bang a rubber ball with one of those paddles that the ball is attached to by a long rubber band (do those things have a name?) like no one else I've ever seen: forehand or backhand, he hit the ball horizontally, vertically, and any angle in between, and he hit it fifteen, twenty, thirty feet, without a miss.

Rolly wasn't fast, as in sprinting, but he was quick, big, powerful, and tough. He got into fights now and then, but he never started one. Tough guys heard that Rolly was tough and wanted to find out for themselves. They found out fast. If they managed to land a hard punch, they were dismayed to find that it didn't even faze him—he could take an amazing amount of pain. But they didn't land many, and after two or three minutes they were a mess—welts, bruises, cuts, a lot of blood—while Rolly was hardly marked. I felt safe in his company.

Always talkative, Jack had a gift for telling tall-tales, aka bullshit; always terse, Rolly had a gift for getting to the point. With girls they were both utterly mute. On Friday and

Saturday nights, instead of going to parties, they liked to go downtown to see what kind of fun they could turn up, for nothing. They didn't believe in paying for anything unless they absolutely had to. As they put it, if you couldn't get it for free—whatever it was—you didn't deserve it, a principle Johnny and I readily subscribed to. On those weekend nights we weren't going to a party, we began joining them.

Taking the bus from different neighborhoods, we would meet downtown at a designated time and place. Often, when we had been hanging out with each other during the day, we would take the bus together. Then the getting there itself was fun. We'd stand in the middle of the floor and, touching nothing with our hands, ride the bus like a surf board. Sometimes we'd sing Stephen Foster and Hank Williams songs with quiet, tremulous, over-done sincerity. Sometimes we'd speak nonsense syllables pretending to be foreigners. We'd laugh at pretend jokes, hmm and tsk tsk at pretend bad news, agree and disagree with pretend observations. We actually believed that the other passengers actually believed that we were actually foreigners.

Once downtown we walked through alleys, slid down and climbed back up delivery chutes, checked doors to see if they were unlocked—if they were, we walked in only to be told by a janitor or a night watchman to get our asses out. Once in a while no one was there, but when that happened there was nowhere to go, either—just a hallway with two or three locked doors, a stairway leading to another locked door, a locked elevator—but it felt exhilarating anyway, being where we weren't supposed to be at that hour, the weird silence of it.

In the alleys we scrounged through trash cans to see what we might find of interest and/or value, and we often scored: magazines, books, notebooks, pens, pencils, calenders, ashtrays, umbrellas, salt and pepper shakers, lipsticks and bottles of nail polish and perfume, fingernail clippers, lamps, clocks, little radios, records, belts, ties, brassieres, slippers, shoes, shirts—it was amazing what people threw away. Most of it we tossed, mainly because we didn't want to carry it around, but some we kept.

We checked cars to see if they were unlocked. If they were, and no one was around to watch, we searched them for money and valuables, and occasionally scored: some loose change occasionally, sometimes a shirt, a couple times a little transistor radio, once a camera.

Walking along the sidewalks we'd sometimes bust out into song and dance, jumping up and down steps and curbs, swinging around street signs, leapfrogging over parking meters. Some bystanders would laugh, some shake their heads in bemused disbelief, and others pretend not to notice. We wanted to see if anyone would join us, the way they do in movie musicals, but no one—not one—ever did.

We always checked out the concession stands in the lobbies of various buildings—the First National Bank, the National Bank of Tulsa, the Philtower, the Kennedy, the Mayo, the Thompson, the Mid-Continent, the Atlas Life, the Petroleum, the Stanolind. The concessions were closed at night, but we'd see if we could snitch something—candy, pop, pastries—from the vending machines. We rarely succeeded, but we always tried. (You never could tell.) We checked pay phones and scouted the sidewalks for change.

We really liked the hotels—the Mayo, the Adams, the Bliss, the Alvin Plaza, the Hotel Tulsa—because they were open and we could roam around them virtually at will. We'd find an unoccupied conference room and turn on the lights, check out the art on the walls (which we usually found wanting but, oddly enough, we never defaced), mess around with intercom systems, push each other around in desk chairs with wheels, play shuffleboard with thick glass ashtrays on the long tables, and we'd dance on the tables, too. If there was a dinner-dance type of affair in a ballroom, with middle-aged folks and a society band, we'd watch for a while and wonder what in hell they had to laugh about so much and how in God's name they could enjoy such anemic music. If there was a more informal do with a buffet, we'd

54 *Low Crimes and Misdemeanors*

go in and quickly snatch some of the chow before we got kicked out.

When we got hungry, we went to Michael's, a popular cafeteria on Boulder. We went there because of the layout: two front doors, one on the south side, the other on the north. You entered the south side, walked to the back of the room where the food was laid out, picked out your meal as you went across, and got your bill from a woman at the end of the line. After eating you paid a cashier stationed at the north door and exited. At least that was the theory. But we would eat, then exit via the south door, the entrance, thus skipping the cashier and getting our meal for nothing. That simple.

Often, to cap off our night on the town, we'd go see a movie. To get into the Orpheum, the Rialto, the Ritz, the Majestic, the Tulsa (and neighborhood theaters as well: the Royal, the Delman, the Will Rogers, the Brookside), we'd check the exit doors to see if any were open. Usually they weren't, but once in a while one was and we'd slip in. More often one of us would go into the lobby and tell the usher he was looking for his sister (or brother or cousin). In the auditorium he would walk up and down the aisles pretending to be looking for her, then, during a scene that was dark, slip through the heavy curtains of an exit and open the door to let the others in. He would slip back out into the auditorium, pretend to look some more, then return to the lobby, tell the usher he couldn't find her, go back out and around to the exit door where the rest of us would let him in, then we'd all sneak into the auditorium.

One night Johnny and I found the exit door to the Brookside Theater unlocked. We slid in and inched our way through the dark tunnel to the heavy curtain, then peeked out into the auditorium. It was almost empty—seven or eight customers scattered around, and several ushers sitting together in the back. Worse yet, the movie was a western featuring a sky so bright we could see the color of the ushers' hair. We couldn't get into the auditorium without being noticed. It was like cracking a safe only to find it empty. But we couldn't just leave as if we had never been there. So we did the only thing we could think of: behind the screen we ran across the stage and back, stomping as hard and hollering as loud as we could, and then we made our exit into the night.

The Ritz Theater was the easiest to get into. The usher taking the tickets—always a frail senior-citizen type, it seemed—was stationed on the far side of the concession stand, an arrangement as vulnerable as the one at Michael's. We'd walk into the lobby when it was busy between shows, buy a Coke (yes, I know, we paid for the Coke, but as a cover, a legitimate means to an illegitimate end, and besides, everyone has to compromise once in a while), then, Coke in hand, we'd walk past the usher. If he asked for our tickets, we'd tell him we had just come out to get a drink and were going back in, and no, we didn't have our ticket stubs, so? and the poor guy wasn't about to challenge several strapping teenage boys. That ploy worked for several years, but one night we walked into the lobby only to see a cop standing by the usher, whereupon we walked right back out. Our jig was up.

### Cherokee Bill

In grade school my friends and I went every Saturday to the matinee at the Royal Theater on East Eleventh. When we started junior high, though, we put such childish things as Saturday matinees behind us. Then we went to the Royal only occasionally, to see a specific movie or to hustle a necking session with any girl we could find—and any girl would do—who came for the same reason. One Friday night, though, Johnny, Jack, Rolly, and I actually paid to see a show because we didn't want to chance missing it. It wasn't a movie; rather, it was the sharp-shooter Cherokee Bill.

We expected a full house, but for some reason only a

few people showed up. We sat in the second row. After giving up on late-comers, the manager finally came out and, reading from a sheet of paper, introduced the best shot in the entire world, civilized and uncivilized alike, straight from his tour of all the major European capitals, the amazing genius with a firearm as well as every other weapon known to man, the one and only Cherokee Bill!

Then out popped this gaunt old guy with a rifle in his left hand and a bull whip in his right. He was wearing a Kelly-green, sequin-bedecked cowboy suit, a white Stetson out of which gray stringy hair hung down to his shoulders (at a time when no man wore hair over his ears), and cowboy boots with silver toes and heels. He had a manic, somewhat demented gleam in his eye and a motor mouth that rapidly cracked corny one-liners as rapidly as Henny Youngman, as Robin Williams, but without the humor. While the rest of the audience (the few) sat in stunned disbelief, the four of us started guffawing loudly, until Bill stopped, pointed his rifle directly at Jack and me, and said, "You two!" Jack and I pointed at ourselves with a "*Moi*?" expression on our faces. "That's right, you two smartasses! Git up here, now!" We pointed at the stage with an "Up there?" expression on our faces. "That's right: up here! Now!"

Jack and I stood up. Rolly and John said, "Don't! Are you guys crazy? He's nuts!" But that was the reason we were moving toward the aisle—he was nuts, and we were afraid not to obey. We walked up the steps onto the stage. He lashed the whip at me—it loudly snapped in mid-air, then the end wrapped gently around my waist. He yanked me to the center of the stage and ordered me to stay there. He flicked his whip free, then lashed it around Jack, yanked him to a spot near me, ordered him to stay there, and flicked his whip free. Then he laid his rifle on a table, picked up a newspaper and gave it to us, instructing us to hold it between us. Facing the audience, he stepped back about twenty feet, took aim, then swung the whip over-armed and sliced the newspaper in half. He told me to drop my half and take the other end of

Jack's. I did. Then he sliced that piece in half, told me to drop my half and take the piece Jack was holding, and sliced it in half. We were now holding a three- or four-inch piece between us, which he also sliced in half.

He laid his whip on the little table and escorted Jack and me to the left side of the stage. He positioned us facing the audience, stuck a six-inch piece of chalk in each of our mouths, and ordered us to stand still. Johnny and Rolly yelled, "Get out of there, you guys! Run!" but we were too scared to move: Cherokee Bill's gleam was now beyond manic; it was maniacal. He walked to the other side of the stage. Out of the corner of my eye I saw him pick up his rifle as Johnny and Rolly were hollering, "No no no!" I turned my eye to the audience, the rifle fired, and the chalk in my mouth poofed into powder. He fired again and Jack's chalk poofed the same. He repeated the stunt with five-inch pieces of chalk, then four.

Next, Cherokee Bill turned me to face the other side of the stage, strapped an apple on top of my head—yes, the old William Tell bit—then walked to the other side of the stage. An apple is much bigger than a cylinder of chalk, granted, but with the chalk I was facing the audience—I couldn't see Bill. Now I could see him, and his rifle, which was aimed at the apple on top of my head. Only it seemed to be pointing straight between my eyes. Which, in a paralysis of terror, I kept open. And stood still. As still as a praying mantis holding its breath and praying its butt off. While Rolly and John were bellowing. Then Cherokee Bill fired and the apple was gone.

But Bill had an even better trick in store. He tied another apple on my head (Why me?!—I didn't know and was afraid to ask.), then crossed back to the other side of the stage, turned his back to me, rested the rifle on his left shoulder, placed his right thumb on the trigger, and stretched out his left arm with a little mirror in his hand, the kind that women carry in their purses. A little mirror that he was aiming with. Unnerving me entirely, but no longer in fear.

No, I was unnerved to the point of having no emotion at all, just a quiet, almost peaceful sense that my time was up and that's the way it goes, first your ass and then your nose, as we used to say. But Cherokee Bill was bang on, thank God, and I lived to tell the tale.

A few years later I ran into a guy who had ushered at the Royal that night. He told me my evening could have been a lot more interesting. Bill could have thrown the knives at me that he'd been practicing with before the show.

### *One Hundred Eighty Proof*

During our junior high school years my buddies and I played baseball in the Peewee League, the Tulsa equivalent at the time of Little League. Because we had sponsors and wore cleats and uniforms (wool, by the way), we felt like we were playing baseball for real, not the kid stuff of grade school Midget League when we wore jeans and tennis shoes. In Midget League I was a force, hitting over five hundred, but when I moved up to Peewee my force fizzled and went flat—suddenly I was a two hundred hitter. Having some testosterone working for them, the pitchers now threw much harder, and they threw curves and sliders and change-ups as well, and I swung and missed. My reputation and my self-esteem shot to shit, I sought redemption in prayer (*Please, God, help me hit a curve ball.*) and in playing extra hard and tough.

One afternoon we ("we" being Glen Dobbs Driving Range, our sponsor) were playing a team with a pitcher who pissed us all off. He was big, a hundred eighty pounds or so, we guessed, and even though a good deal of it was still baby fat, he was formidable because he had a mean fast ball, an ornery curve, and pretty good control. What pissed us off, though, was his style. He played cat-and-mouse, dusting his fingers off with the rosin bag, stepping on the rubber then stepping off and adjusting his cap, then back on to take the signal, shaking it off, shaking off another, stepping back off the rubber to wipe his brow—all to keep the batter off balance, out of rhythm. And it was working. We were all either striking out or hitting feeble grounders. After three innings I decided to give him the same.

Next time I was up I dusted my hands with dirt, stepped into the batter's box, fidgeted around taking my stance, then, just as he was ready to wind up, stepped out to tap the bat against my cleats, stepped back in, fidgeted around some more taking my stance, then just as he was about to wind up I stepped back out to hitch my balls, blow my nose, spit, and so forth. I worked a walk out of him and in the process got him so riled up that he tried to pick me off and threw the ball away. I got to third, then our next guy up smacked a single (our first hit) and scored me, which put us ahead one-zip.

Next inning this same pitcher got a single. The batter after him hit a blooper to right field. As our right fielder charged the ball the pitcher rounded second and headed toward third, where I played, looking straight at me with an expression of resolute, determined, revenge-on-the-brain rage. Our right fielder scooped the ball up and threw it to me, on a line—a perfect peg, I could see, but maybe not in time to reach me before the pitcher would. So, thinking to myself, *C'mon, motherfucker, I'll take you on even if you do weigh fifty pounds more than me*, I positioned myself two feet in front of the bag to block him off. Instead of sliding, he leaped hip first right up into me just as I caught the ball and down I went onto my back as he landed, one hundred eighty pounds of angry baby fat, bone, muscle and all, right on my face.

Oh but it was lovely. Not only had I scored on him and then gotten him out, I had also got my nose broken big-time, scraped and bloody and smashed across my face—proof to the world that, yeah yeah, I wasn't hitting the way I once did, but I was still the scrappy tough guy I liked to think I was.

## *Above and Beyond the Call of Duty*

Hoping a change of teams might make me play better, I switched one season from Glen Dobbs to Cox Motors, a long-established team that always came in first or second because the coach, a middle-aged man everyone called Ham, knew the game inside out. I decided I wanted to try pitching—partly for the challenge, partly as an excuse for a lousy batting average—and Ham said fine. He taught me technique, how to use my whole body to increase my velocity and control and at the same time spare my arm. He also helped me with my batting—a lighter bat, a higher right elbow, a more closed stance—so that when I didn't pitch I often played third.

The irony of my time with Cox was that, after learning how to play with good form, I came down with some ailments I'd never suffered before. My lower back seized up. Dr. Reed prescribed some exercises and a bed board under my mattress. I strained the arch of my right foot, making it painful even to walk, much less pitch. Dr. Reed prescribed arch supports. Then, about halfway through the season, playing third one game, I fielded a grounder and threw the ball to first, only a severe pain ripped through my shoulder and the ball fell thirty feet short. So much for the arm Ham had taught me to spare: I couldn't even lift it. I sat on the bench the next few games to give it a rest, time to heal.

A couple weeks later we were warming up for a night game and I found that as long as I took it very easy, I could throw the ball. Our starting pitcher got off to a shaky start, allowing several hits and four runs the first two innings. Ham pulled him and put in another, who lasted two innings and gave up another three or four. Ham asked me if I could go. We had been scoring ourselves and had a chance to win. Imagining what the Gipper and Audi Murphy and the early Christians would do, I decided to tough out the pain, to sacrifice my arm if necessary for the sake of the team, but (of course) without betraying the least discomfort—in short, to be a hero.

I threw a fastball. It wasn't fast and the batter smacked it for a double. After that I threw nothing but curves, big slow roundhouse curves, the kind that stress the shit out of a shoulder, and they gave the batters fits. For two innings. I had never known such soul-satisfying pain. But then the batters figured out they should wait for the ball to arrive before swinging, and when I say "wait" I mean *wait*. They waited for my pitches the way you wait for a bus, watching it approach three blocks away, then two, then one, looming larger and larger until it arrives and stops right in front of you. And that was when they hit it. Boy oh boyo did they hit it. And we lost. So not only did I sacrifice my arm for the team, I had sacrificed it for a lost cause. And here's the upshot: I didn't feel like a hero or even a martyr; instead, having to clumsily brush my teeth and wipe my toosh for two weeks with my left hand, I felt like a fool.

### *Bully Boy*

In junior high there were also Peewee Leagues for football and basketball. The teams were not officially affiliated with the schools, but they were named after the schools the players went to: Wilson, Cleveland, Roosevelt, etc. (Our junior highs were named after presidents.) Accordingly, my buddies and I played for Wilson. One afternoon before football practice a bunch of us were goofing around, and Johnny, for some obscure adolescent reason, peed in a Dixie cup, then wondered what to do with it. We all agreed he couldn't just throw it away—otherwise why would he have taken the trouble to piss in the cup?—but what were the options? No one dared drink it, although the dare was issued by several, and when Johnny threatened to throw it on someone we all warned him not to or he'd be in the hospital. Then we saw a guy some of us knew walking across the playground. He was our age but slight and rather shy, and he was carrying a violin case, which meant he had victim written all over his person. "I know!" I said: "I'll throw it on him!"

"You sure?" they asked.

"Hell yeah. Gimme that cup." So, happy (as usual) to be the center of attention, I took the cup and approached him. He had a wary, scared look in his eyes. I said, "Hey, Howard, how you doin"?"

"O...kay," he nervously answered, looking at the cup in my hand.

"Oh yeah?" I taunted, and threw the pee on his chest and legs. He stared at me a second, looking humiliated and helpless, but he didn't lose his composure by crying or running. Instead, he started walking again, exactly as he had before, only a little faster. We hooted and jeered a bit, until he rounded a building, passing out of sight and out of mind. Our coach arrived and we practiced as usual.

That night Mom got a call from Vice-Principal Tharp. He told her what I had done, and told her to tell me to see him in his office first thing next morning. She asked me if I had done what he said. I said yes. She said that she was ashamed of me, that she despised bullying and had taught me to, and she hoped to God I felt ashamed of myself. It only took me a moment of reflection—and I hadn't reflected until that moment—to realize, and to say, I did. Then she informed me that as soon as possible we were going to go over to Howard's house and I was going to apologize in person to him and to his parents—whom, by the way, she had known for years—and as of that moment I was grounded for a month. And by grounded she meant no football, no TV, no radio, no phone, no nothing except school. I didn't argue.

Next morning, Mr. Tharp asked me if I would have thrown the pee on Jerry McBride. (Jerry was a hood who also happened to be one of the biggest and toughest guys in school.) I had to admit I wouldn't have. He asked me if I was proud of myself. I admitted I wasn't. He asked me if I was ever going to do such a thing again. I said no. (And I didn't.) He asked me how my mother was punishing me. I told him.

He said he couldn't do anything that would make my punishment any worse, so he would let me go, but with a warning: he better not see me in his office again for any reason or I'd be on the street. Did I understand? I understood.

The meeting with Howard and his parents made me feel like unadulterated dog shit, because it was obvious how thoroughly humiliated he felt—so helpless against a bully like me—and yet he and they had the grace not only to thank me for my apology, but even to wish me well.

It was a long month.

### *Quick and Mean*

When I tried out for the junior high football team, I had visions of playing halfback, of making electrifying runs and scoring game-winning touchdowns, but C. B. Stanley, the coach, decided to start me at left tackle. I pointed out that I wasn't lineman size. "With the offense we're gonna run, the split-T," he explained, "a lineman doesn't have to be all that big, just quick and mean, and that's you, Red Hoss," he smiled, putting an arm around my shoulder, "quick and mean." Well, armed with the name *Red Hoss* and those two adjectives, *quick* and *mean*, I decided to make the best of the position and quickly found I enjoyed it. It was a kick lining up face-to-face with guys who at first regarded me as a snack before they devoured the runner, but then I hit them right at the count and before they knew it, the runner was past them. With every game I was feeling quicker and meaner.

One game we played a team that had a left tackle who weighed about two hundred sixty pounds. For junior high even today that's big, but for junior high in the early fifties it was monstrous. Our right tackle—who in my opinion was a little short in the muscle and balls department—couldn't move him, so I suggested a play in which I would run down the line and take him out from the side—a surprise flank attack. He was slow as a slug, so I knew that with my Red-Hoss quickness and meanness I could mow that big sack of fat down and out. At the count I charged down the line and into his gut helmet-first. Instantly I was looking up at the sky and he was on top of me and the runner, both of us groaning and telling him to get the fuck off. "That's okay, Red Hoss," C. B. said in the next timeout, "he's a freak. We'll just have to run around him."

On defense C. B. had me playing right end, again on account of my quickness and meanness, he said. My main job was to turn sweeps in—i.e., to keep whoever was running with the ball from getting outside of me. I didn't have to tackle him, although of course I could, but that was extra credit. Most of the time I did a decent job, even made a good number of tackles, but one game I remember especially well because in it I... Well, read on.

It was in our ninth grade year; we were playing the B team (i.e., the junior varsity, tenth grade) from Broken Arrow. A suburb of Tulsa now, back then Broken Arrow was a small blue-collar town whose denizens looked on Tulsa—affluent, Republican, white-collar Tulsa—as a city populated by nose-in-the-air effetes who used words like *affluent* and *denizen* and *effete*, and therefore needed some heavy put-down. We had especially looked forward to this game because it was against guys a year older than us and it was scheduled for night, making us feel big-time.

We got the kickoff and they tore our blitzkrieg split-T offense apart in three plays. We had gained minus fifteen yards. We punted, tackled their receiver after holding him to a forty yard return, then found ourselves facing one of the oldest-fashioned offensive formations around, the single-wing. Out of the twenties, for God's sake. Knute Rockne jive. On their first play they ran up the middle and made a couple yards. On their second play they ran a sweep my way, three backs in front of the runner. I set myself to turn the runner in, but wham! two of the backs plowed into me, one high, the other low, and not only did their runner zip around me and rip off twenty yards, they had discovered our team's weak spot. Me. They ran every other play at me—no exaggeration—and they crushed me every single time. Not once did I turn the runner in, much less make a tackle. I didn't cower, exactly, but if I could have dug a foxhole to take cover in, I would have. To make my humiliation worse, I could see the contempt and glee in their faces as they came charging my way, anticipating the pleasure of pulverizing me, my macho adjectives, my self-image, and my self-esteem yet again.

"Well, Red Hoss," C. B. told me after the game, "tonight you got a good ole-fashioned ass-whuppin', pure and simple."

"I guess I wasn't quick and mean enough," I joked.

"Oh, there's no guess about it," he said, then threw an arm around my neck, Dutch-rubbed my head with his knuckles, and said, "but you did your darndest, and you're my Red Hoss just the same."

It was small consolation, but it was the only consolation around, and I took it.

### *Crowder*

Billy. He lived up on the next block. His house was on one side of a double lot. At the back of the other side was his dad's shop, a corrugated metal structure the size of a small barn where Mr. Crowder did some kind of business with machine parts when he wasn't slowly cruising around on his big Harley or taking a dip in the large round galvanized stock tank near his shop. In front of the shop Billy used to drive a little motor scooter around and around a dirt track he had worn in the grass, practicing tricks: riding in a squat now on the left side and now on the right, picking a hat up off the ground while driving by it, standing on one foot leaning forward with his other foot stretched out behind him like an ice-skater, then on the other foot the same. He did trick-riding exhibitions at motorcycle races, he got so good.

In grade school I didn't hang with Billy much. Wiry and extremely strong, he was always getting into fights and other trouble at school—I liked that—but he didn't play baseball, football, or basketball, and at home he was always riding his damn motor scooter. When junior high began his dad sent him to military school for an attitude adjustment. When Billy came home for Christmas and summer with his old attitude still alive and kicking, we became buddies.

The Christmas of seventh grade we had a nice snow. I took him over to Johnny's to introduce him to our favorite winter pastime, which I have waited until now to describe because Billy immediately became the center of it, the star. When we told him what we were going to do, he said what I had said when John first told me about it: "You're shittin' me." He didn't believe it simply because it sounded too good to be true. We said, "You'll see, butthook; you'll see."

Johnny got bundled up and we went to the nearest corner with a stop sign. We hid behind some bushes. When the first car came to a stop, we slipped behind it, grabbed the bumper and squatted on our haunches. The car took off and, because we were wearing slick-soled boots, we slid right along behind. It was sort of like water skiing without skis. Being so close to the surface and in the open air, fifteen miles an hour felt like thirty, twenty like forty, and twenty-five like flight. Like me the first time, Billy could hardly believe he was doing what we were doing, it was so simple, so foolhardy and wrong and illegal, so much fun. We hitched rides all day until dark.

What made car-hitching possible was that Tulsa had no snow removal. The snow on the streets became packed, and we rode all over town, even on thoroughfares like East Eleventh. But Billy took car-hitching to new levels. Instead of waiting for cars to stop, he caught them on the run, sprinting after them, leaping and grabbing the bumper with two hands, or just one, pulling himself up to the bumper while being dragged until he could squat. We did the same as best we could, but we had neither his speed nor his strength, so he caught rides that were beyond us.

When Rolly and Jack got in on the action, Billy introduced fighting to the sport: we'd try to knock each other off, pounding each other's hands, hacking each other's wrists, elbowing and hipping each other, even in traffic on busy streets. When someone got knocked off, he'd somehow slide and roll to the curb. After a thaw and a refreeze, we would hit patches of bare pavement that would yank our legs out from beneath us. Sometimes we'd hit ice again quickly enough to pull ourselves back up to a squat, but sometimes not: we'd lose our grip and roll. Riding behind four-door cars we would sometimes work our way around to the side of the car, grab the back-door handle and pull ourselves up to it, then grab the front-door handle and pull ourselves up to it, then stand up and give the driver a shit-fit.

Remarkably enough, we never got stopped by the cops, nor did any of us ever get hurt. Go figure.


### *Motor Sports*

Billy's dad was a worrywart, constantly yelling, "Billy, be careful! Don't do that, son! Watch out, Billy!" and the like, yet he gave Billy the motor scooter when he was eight, a three-quarter size midget racing car when he was eleven, and a full-size Harley when he was thirteen. A radically mixed message, to be sure, but Billy radically un-mixed it, disregarding the warnings and driving the machines with wild abandon, doing those stunts on the scooter, and roaring around the neighborhood in the racing car, bouncing off curbs and sometimes winding up in a driveway, or even a yard.

He let me drive it. It had a clutch that you depressed two inches, a four-speed transmission so small that you just nudged the stick between your legs from one gear to the next, and steering so tight that you turned the wheel only a tad to take a corner. The car was so low you couldn't roll it, which meant you could spin into terrific one-eighties and, with a little gravel or sand on the street, even three-sixties. I can't say why no one ever called the cops; all I know is we never got busted for recklessly driving a loud illegal uninsured vehicle without a driver's license.

And the motorcycle. Summer days and nights Billy and I often tooled around on it, him in front driving, usually, me in back riding, but sometimes the other way around. The Harleys back then didn't have a hand-clutch and a foot-shift; instead, they had a hand-shift on the right side of the gas tank and a foot-clutch on the left. The clutch was what they called a rocking-chair. It had two connected pedals, front and back. Instead of letting it go to release it, like a car's clutch, you had to push the front pedal down with your toe; to engage it you pushed the back pedal down with your heel—thus the name rocking-chair. It was a safety feature: you weren't as likely to lose control taking off because your foot couldn't accidentally slip off the clutch.

Billy's headlight was feeble and his brakes iffy. The headlight wasn't important when we were driving around town at night—the street lamps and the car lights provided plenty of illumination—but when we sped sixty-five, seventy miles an hour at night on the roads winding through Mohawk Park and could see only ten, fifteen yards ahead of us, well, that was hairy. We drove fast in town—up to sixty, sometimes—and when the brakes didn't catch, we'd weave back and forth, leaning far enough to make the footrests scrape the pavement, to help us slow down. If we couldn't stop before running into something, we'd turn into driveways, go up curbs, spin to a stop in parking lots or yards.

In time Billy souped his Harley up (way up) and installed a suicide clutch—i.e., a clutch that worked like a car clutch, making it more dangerous but much better for quick starts. He also installed a new headlight and new brakes. He got a flame job on the tanks. He put on resonating pipes without mufflers, which made for a sound very deep, brawny, rich, and so loud you could hear him coming a full block away. Every summer through junior high we drove this wild-ass machine like lunatics in town and out, not only without getting into a wreck, but also, mystifyingly enough, without getting a ticket for speeding, for reckless driving, for driving without a license, for driving an unregistered unlicensed uninsured vehicle, for illegal pipes—for anything!

That much luck just doesn't seem right.


## *The Mechanic*

Johnny got a Cushman motor scooter. Cushmans had small fat wheels, a platform for the driver's feet, a motor beneath the seat, and behind the seat a small trunk with a cushioned lid that a passenger could sit on. Johnny kept some wrenches and screwdrivers in his trunk because his scooter had a habit of randomly stalling. He would pull over, park the scooter on its kick stand, open the trunk and pull out his tools, lift off the seat, study the engine a bit, then go to work with wrenches and screwdriver. After tinkering a bit he would put his tools back into the trunk, replace the seat, kick-start the motor, which always came right back to life, and break into a smug complacent grin.

"C'mon, John," we'd say, "who're you kiddin'? You're not doin' a damned thing. You don't know jack-shit about engines."

Johnny would shoot us a look of pained superiority— the genius having to deal with the unwashed, untutored mob—and say, "It's runnin', ain't it?" A matter of fact we couldn't dispute, but we still weren't convinced.

Then one day Johnny, Jack, Rolly, and I were hanging around at Jack's house. Jack lived on a rutted, potholed dirt road. Johnny was driving his scooter back and forth in front of the house. The motor would stall, Johnny would go through his repair routine, kick-start the motor, take off, and within seconds it would stall again. Rolly, Jack, and I were amused; Johnny was not. His repair routine was obviously not working—indeed, it was blowing his cover—and he didn't know what to do. (Neither did we, but we never pretended we did.) After about half an hour a kid nine or ten years old, who'd been watching this show the whole time, said, "Hey, buddy, the problem is—"

Johnny interrupted: "Just mind your own business, kid."

"But I—"

"I said, mind your own fuckin' business."

The three of us chimed in: "Give him a chance, John. Let him talk. He might know somethin' you don't."

"Bullshit," Johnny said. "He's a kid!"

"So tell *us*," we said to the kid.

"Every time he hits a bump, that metal plate on the bottom of his seat hits the spark plug and grounds the engine out."

"So if he'd just take the metal plate off he wouldn't have any problem?" Jack asked.

"Right," the kid said. "Simple as pie."

"You hear that, Johnny?" Rolly said as we whooped and hollered with laughter. "Simple as pie. Now thank the kid."

"Aaaa, go fuck yourselves," Johnny growled, and, standing on the platform in an awkward crouch, he drove away.

The next time we saw him, we asked to see the seat bottom. He told us once again what we could do with ourselves. But we couldn't fail to notice that his engine never stalled again.


### *The Swimming Hole*

On Yale a little south of Thirty-First, there was a field with a pond that Johnny, Jack, Rolly, and I liked to swim in. (Not Billy, though: he preferred to ride his motorcycle around, or to stay at home and work on it.) We never knew who owned it, and whoever it was never bothered us.

You couldn't see the pond from the street because it was set back twenty or thirty yards and it had a four or five foot berm around it. We'd crawl through the barbed-wire fence, step carefully through the random clumps of cow flop, sometimes walk around a cow or two, go over the bank, peel off our duds down to our bathing suits or down to nil, and dive in. Once in a great while others would already be there, and sometimes they'd be skinny-dipping, and once the skinny-dippers were girls who shooed us back over the berm so they could get their swim suits on. But we didn't leave right away. No, we hung around a while, sitting on the bank and hoping for a glimpse of tit and tush and maybe even better, while they treaded water. They issued commands and appeals, we laughed, they laughed then issued more commands and appeals, and so on back and forth until, wanting to get into the water (for there were no trees to sit under, and in the afternoons the temperature often topped a hundred), we finally gave in.

On the surface the water was warmish, but ten, twelve feet down it was cold, and the mud on the bottom was remarkably soft and ankle deep. As nice as it was, the second summer we went swimming there we began to get impatient with it. I mean, there was the water, and some water lilies, and it was cold and muddy at the bottom, and there was the berm to sit on, but that was it. We wanted something to do there. We decided to build a diving board.

On Johnny's Cushman and our bicycles we hauled lumber and tools to the pond. We had to make a number of trips. Several times he towed one of us with a rope. One evening his dad told Johnny and me how he was driving on Thirty-First that afternoon and saw ahead of him some fool kid on a motor scooter with some lumber between his legs towing another fool kid on a bicycle with a long board over the handlebars, and he was wondering what kind of parents would let their kids do anything that stupid and dangerous until he saw that the kids were us. "Don't do that anymore, boys," he said, "cause if yall get hurt or killed, you'll make the Mrs. and me look bad. Ruin our reputations." We laughed and promised we wouldn't, but we did.

We constructed a triangulated structure out of two-by-fours. We drove the long exposed ends into the berm. We shored this structure up with big rocks from the field. We fitted the twelve foot long two-by-twelve into a two-foot-deep slot at the back of the structure, then nailed it down. We laid it between two upright two-by-fours at the fulcrum, a design touch we were proud of because the two-by-fours would keep the board from bouncing sideways off the fulcrum. We nailed burlap bags over the top of the two-by-twelve for secure footing. After working on it for a week or so we were done.

We drew straws to see who would get to "break it in," as we put it. Rolly won. Imitating an Olympic diver, he took three prissy steps to the end of the board, jumped up, landed, and with a very loud crack! the board broke at the fulcrum and Rolly plunged straight down into the pond. At first we were shocked and dismayed: a week of work destroyed on the first jump. Then Jack said, "By God, Rolly, you broke it in, alright!" and we had a laugh.

Nailing the broken-off piece of two-by-twelve across the structure, we devised a platform to jump off of. It was better than nothing, but it was a far cry from a diving board. The following summer McClure's Pool opened up at the east end of town, a very nice facility with three aluminum diving boards, and that was all she wrote for the swimming hole.

### *Diving*

The first summer at McClure's some older guys I admired—Don Brooks, Ralph Chesser, Ben Walcott, and Johnny's older brother Jack—were all there one day, doing front and back flips off the high board, and to my surprise Rolly and Jack were doing them too. Jack's brother Ben asked me if I was going to try one. I said no. He then uttered the deadly words: "Why not, Jeff? You chicken?" Now, I was willing to dive—I'd been doing straight dives off of high boards since I was nine or ten, and bouncing the board too, not just falling off the end head-first—but flips? Off of a board ten feet high? "I'm no fool," I said to myself, but Ben's words burned every time I thought of them, and I thought of them often. "You chicken?" I also thought of how Rolly and Jack didn't say a word. I wanted to crawl under a bed.

A few days later my family and I took a trip to California. One afternoon we visited some friends of friends in Tulsa. In the back yard they had a swimming pool with a dinky little diving board that was maybe eighteen inches off the water—perfect for learning how to do flips on. I spent the afternoon working on them, front and back. I couldn't get enough spring to turn a complete somersault, but by the end of the afternoon I knew that off of a higher, springier board I could, with ease. Better yet, from landing on my back and on my belly, I found that the pain wasn't as bad as I had imagined. In a way I enjoyed it—it proved I wasn't a chicken after all.

Back in Tulsa I joined Rolly and Jack at McClure's first thing. I tried my two flips off the three-foot board. The first few times I landed on my back and my belly, but that was alright because I was displaying my toughness, not to mention my strength of character. After I did the flips successfully a few times, I told Rolly and Jack I was ready for the high board. They gave me some tips on the adjustments I had to make for the greater height. Again I messed up a few times, and let me tell you, landing wrong from twelve feet $(10 + x \ [x = vs \ (vertical \ spring) \ (vs = 2 \ ) \ (x = 2)] = 12 \ )$ hurt a helluva lot more than from five feet $(3 + ditto)$, but the extra pain was worth it, to prove just how truly tough and gutsy I was, and in short order I was doing both flips off the high board successfully.

Soon Johnny joined our adventures in diving, and before long we were all doing front and back flips, jackknives, swans, backdives, cut-aways, half-twists, half-gainers, full gainers, front one-and-a-halfs, and back one-and-a-halfs with a half-twist. Lest I give the wrong impression, let me point out that our twists were crooked, our tucks and pikes loose, and our entries slanted and splashy with knees bent and feet far apart. But we didn't care. All we wanted was to do the dive, fuck the form.

Another idea was to lure acquaintances into a game of follow-the-leader, starting them with the easy stuff, then leading them to the point where they would cop out. It was a cheap way of feeling superior, I know, but what can I say?— we were cheap.

There was one dive we did with fine form—the Frederickson, aka the watermelon. It served the same purpose as the cannonball—to make a big splash—but it was to the cannonball what a stick of dynamite is to a firecracker, what a lake is to a pond, what a Chianti is to a Boone's Farm, what a filet is to a meatball, what a... you get the idea. The cannonball you tucked and landed butt-first, sending a messy splash all over any old where. The Frederickson you tucked at the last split-second as you were entering the water head-first, and if you were heading straight down and you timed your tuck just right, instead of a kersplat and a splash, your entry went *ka-whump*, not loud but kinda deep and resonant, like the concussion of a cannon without the blast, and the spray shot straight up like a geyser. Fat Jack was the master of the Frederickson (another bootless skill in his repertoire)—he would consistently send the spray straight up twenty, twenty-five feet high, a perfect fountain.

One night we saw a guy we'd never seen before do something we'd never seen before. He took the three slow pointy-toe steps that serious divers do, jumped up for the spring, missed the board with his right foot and fell over the side, awkwardly somersaulting as he fell and flopping into the water. We ran over to lend him a hand, only to watch him rise from the bottom and pop through the surface laughing— at us and at the success of his trick dive. We asked him how he did it. It was simple. When you missed the board with your right foot, if you just relaxed you would automatically turn a somersault and hit the water feet-first. If you didn't relax, you'd land smack on your side. We had no trouble relaxing, and we instantly made that dive part of our repertoire.

We liked to charge off the high board in a row hard on each others' heels fanning out just enough not to land on each other. We liked to plunge into the pool in pairs, one guy riding on another's shoulders and either separateing midway down or plunging into the water together, jumping in feet-first, diving in head-first. The guards blew their whistles and hollered at us, and occasionally made us leave the pool for an hour or two, or a day, but they never succeeded in making us stop.

As important as it was to be daring and tough, we did allow a limit, and I was the one who found it. One day Jack told me he could now do a forward double and asked if I would try it. I figured that if Jack said he could do it, he probably could (though you had to be careful with Jack, he was such a tale-teller), and his challenge scared me, because doing a double seemed twice as hard as doing a one-and-a-half, but I couldn't say no for obvious reasons. I only stipulated that he go first, so I could see him actually do it rather than take his word for it.

He walked out to the end of the high board and began bouncing. Now, at the time Jack was about five-three and weighed in at one eighty, so he was a butterball, but he had remarkable balance. He could bounce for five minutes and land in the exact same place at the exact same angle every time (yet another profitless skill in his collection). So he bounced up and down a dozen times or so to get as much height as he could, then launched himself into the air, grabbed his knees and tucked as tightly as he could, which wasn't very tight given the size of his paunch, and he stayed in that position until he hit the water just as he completed two somersaults. When he surfaced I hollered my admiration.

It was my turn. Jack and I went up the stairs together. I stood at the back of the board. Jack asked, "You just gonna bounce once?"

"Yeah. I tuck tighter than you, spin faster, so once should do it."

"I hope you're right," he said.

"Me too," I agreed.

I took a few seconds to get myself psyched and focused, stepped to the end of the board and jumped as high as I could, came down on it as hard as I could, sprang off as high as I could, tucked as tight as I could to spin as fast as I could, and as I was spinning I got lost. I knew I was going to make two complete somersaults with no trouble, but I couldn't tell when I should open. As it turned out, I shouldn't have opened at all, because when I had completed my second spin and opened, I was two or three feet above the water. I can still remember the impact, the sickening whap of my face slamming into the surface and the awful sting of it. I blacked out for an instant, then came to. I slowly swam to the edge, where Jack, who had dove in right behind me, helped me get out. I sat on the edge.

"Jesus, Jeff, you okay?"

"Not so hot, Jack."

The pool was silent. I could feel people staring at me. My face hurt. Jack said, "My God, you busted all your pimples! They're bleeding!" My tongue hurt. I felt something solid but sort of soft and very small in my mouth. I spit it out. Jack said, "Holy shit, Jeff: your tongue's bleeding." He picked up the bit I had spit out. "Jesus! It's the tip of your tongue!" My head was beginning to ache, and my stomach was getting queasy.

"I'm think I'm gonna go home," I said.

"That's probably a good idea," he said.

I went into the locker room and changed, took the bus home, and went to bed.

I didn't stop diving with my buddies, but I never tried

the double again, and they didn't question my machismo for declining to give it another shot. How could they? They wouldn't try it themselves, which was also okay—no blame, no aspersions cast, no calling into question courage or character. The double was Jack's, all Jack's, and we gladly let him have all the glory.

### *Filling Time*

When the lot of us were hanging around in someone's house waiting to do something—to go to the Y, to go swim at McClure's, to go see a movie, to go watch or play baseball or basketball or football—we'd fill the time a number of ways. We'd thumb wrestle. We'd arm wrestle. We'd leg wrestle, where you lie side by side facing opposite ways, lift adjacent legs up and hook them by the knees and then push to see who can turn the other over. We'd Indian wrestle, where you stand with the outside of your front foot against the outside of your opponent's front foot, grab his hand, and push and pull to make him lose his balance before he makes you lose yours.

We had tests of skill that didn't involve strength. Who could juggle three baseballs the longest. Who could chug a pitcher of water the fastest. Who could do the most yoyo tricks. Who could balance a broom on his fingertip the longest. On his chin the longest. Who could throw the most playing cards out of fifty-two into a hat across the room. Who could, while balancing on one foot, pick up a paper bag with his teeth—whoever could pick the bag up folded the lowest without falling over was the winner.

We also had torture tests. Who could hold himself at half-mast in a pushup the longest. Who could stand still in a crouch the longest. Who could hold his breath the longest. Who could hold a pencil at arm's length the longest. Who could take the continuous tapping of a finger tip against breast bone the longest. Who could take a sharp knuckle jabbing a triceps the longest.

When it was an issue of skill and skill alone, Jack usually won. When it was an issue of pain and pain alone, Rolly always won. When strength was involved, Billy, who was a very good wrestler, always won, even though he was the smallest. Though he wasn't exactly small: at sixteen Billy stood five eight, weighed one fifty-five, had an eighteen-inch neck and a twenty-eight inch waist, started every morning with one hundred deep pushups, and could do more than thirty one-handed pushups on either hand. His strength used to drive us nuts. He would grab your wrist, and whatever you did—twist and jerk, hit his hand, beat it, kick it, smash it against a door frame, bite it—you couldn't break his grip. What made it worse, he laughed at you the whole time.

Billy had another pain-maker he was fond of, what he called the horse bite. He'd grab your inner thigh and squeeze his four fingers into the heel of his hand with a big chunk of your meat in between, which hurt bad enough, but then he'd rip his hand free like a tackler tearing the ball out of a running back's arm, which hurt even worse.

One day Johnny announced that he'd learned a new way to inflict pain, with a pinch so deadly that it not only hurt like hell, it left a long-lasting, deep, dark bruise, a hickey of sorts. He demonstrated it on me. Taking a bit of skin on top of my bicep between the knuckles of his first and second fingers, Johnny squeezed the skin by pressing his thumb into the knuckle of his first finger, then suddenly twisted the skin hard. It hurt, and sure enough, in a matter of seconds a dark bruise appeared. Gloating a little over the damage he'd done, Johnny announced, "And that, my friends, was just an easy-does-it sample." Then he turned to Billy: "Okay, Crowder, tell you what: I'll do my pinch on your arm, then you do your horse bite on mine."

"Fine by me," Billy said.

Now, you have to understand that while Billy's strength drove us all nuts, it drove Johnny just about apoplectic. Johnny was very competitive, and to lose to someone every single time was simply unacceptable. So we could tell by the grin on his face that he thought—thought? he *knew*—that finally he was going to beat Billy at his own game.

Johnny went first. "On the count of three, alright?" he asked.

"Fine by me," Billy answered.

Johnny grasped some skin on Billy's bicep with his knuckles, the same as he did me, then, with the smirk of Wiley Coyote when he thinks he's got Road Runner in the bag, he counted. On three Billy flexed and muscle instantly displaced epidermis, leaving Johnny empty-knuckled. There was nothing to pinch. His smirk turned into an expression of disbelieving despair. Rolly, Jack, and I fell on the floor, we were laughing so hard. Johnny managed a grin, but verily, it was a shit-eating grin.

"Now it's my turn," Billy said, and with such anticipation and menace that Rolly, Jack, and I said, "Uh oh." He took a handful of Johnny's upper arm, the tender inner side, then counted. On "three" he squeezed and ripped. Johnny took it stoically—he wasn't about to give Billy the satisfaction of even a wince—but the rest of us moaned and laughed. Across the inside of Johnny's arm were four thick stripes that a child might have finger-painted, only they were bloody scratches.

Johnny turned to Billy and said, "Now we're even, buttface."

And you know, in a way they were.


## A Day at the Tulsa County Fair

It was in the fall of 1954 at Will Rogers High School B-squad football practice that five tacklers ended up on Rolly's leg and he hobbled up the hill on his own to the locker room to shower and dress, and as he waited for his folks he watched his leg swell to such a size that the trainer slit his jeans to mid-thigh and his folks took him straight to the hospital where x-rays revealed a fractured femur and he got a cast from thigh top to ankle plus a pair of aluminum elbow crutches. His season was shot. The bunch of us still went out together, but we didn't sneak in anywhere because Rolly couldn't. And when we went to the County Fair that year, we didn't do any rides.

We went to a few shows: a variety show; the motor-cycle show where two guys did tricks riding around horizon-tally in a large steel cylinder; the freak show where for an extra fifty cents we got to see the morphodite. (In case you haven't guessed, that was our word for hermaphrodite). We played the various tossing games—coins into bottles, rings over bottles, ping-pong balls into a bowl, softballs into a tilted basket, baseballs into stacked bottles, beanbags into holes in a tilted board, darts into balloons; we did the shoot-ing galleries, including the horse races where you shoot a water gun at a target to make your horse move; and we did those aquariums where you try to pick up cheap plastic trinkets—rings and pens and watches and little binoculars and such—with steam shovel jaws that you operate by turning a little wheel and that Rolly was actually good at.

At a bottle toss, to great applause from bystanders, I won a four-foot teddy bear that I announced I was going to give to this girl I was interested in. I had heard she was at the fair, and with this bear, who knows, I might be able to rack up some points. I walked around the midway looking for her with no luck, and when I walked by the game again the barker offered me a deal: take another chance and bet the bear against twenty-five bucks. Some bystanders urged me to go for it, others warned me not to, but I needed neither encouragement nor discouragement to decide what to do. I had won before, ergo I could win again, and thus I could have the bear plus twenty-five bucks. But of course I lost: lost the money I put down to play, lost the bear, and lost my luster in the public eye, turning from a winner into a sucker that everyone laughed at. And five minutes later, who shows up but the girl I had been looking for, to collect the prize she'd heard about. She came in a glow, she left in a huff, our relationship nipped in the bud.

After running out of money, Jack, Johnny, Billy, Rolly, and I went behind the midway and sprawled on the top of a ridge to rest and shoot the breeze and enjoy the warm, sunny, September afternoon. After a while we saw a few people about twenty-five yards away walking toward us along the path on the ridge top. Johnny jumped up, grabbed Rolly's crutches and, holding one leg stiff, hobbled toward the people. When they were a few yards apart, Johnny slipped and fell, tumbling down the slope screaming and holding his leg. The people rushed down the hill in a panic, yelling, "Oh my God! Oh, you poor thing! Oh sweet Jesus!" and the like, until they reached him and found that he was actually laughing.

They weren't amused, but we were, and we spent the next two hours watching Johnny pull the same stunt over and over, falling every bit as spectacularly as Chevy Chase, as Chris Farley—rolling, flipping, flopping, skidding on his belly, on his back, on his side, punishing himself to make his falls look real because, like all clowns, Johnny was willing to suffer a lot to get a laugh. Some people enjoyed his joke, others resented it, still others dismissed it with a shrug as adolescent silliness, but the five of us found it unfailingly and absolutely funny. And for a bonus, I forgot all about the girl I would never get anywhere with.

### *Scalping*

Late summer of 1954, Jack Nilson and Don Brooks told Johnny and me, along with Rolly and Jack, of a great way to make money. They had graduated from high school and were leaving town for college, so they would no longer be doing it themselves and we wouldn't be competing. *It* was scalping tickets at Tulsa University football games.

We worked in pairs. Each pair worked one of the two

corner gates on Eleventh, because they were the busiest. One guy called out, "Extra tickets? Any extra tickets?" There were always some who had extras—T.U. had mediocre teams at the time—and after some good-natured haggling, they often sold them to us at a bargain price. Some even gave us their extras. The one who got the tickets gave them to his partner, who called out, "Tickets here! Who needs tickets?" We haggled with those who did and settled on a price that was good for them—less than gate value—and good for us, a win/win deal that made everyone happy.

We switched our pairings around from game to game to equalize income and thus prevent jealousy and resentment. All of us could wheel and deal, but some were better than others. As a rule, Rolly was the least effecttive because he was so shy, but that first year was the year he got his leg busted, so, getting and selling while tottering around on crutches, he had the sympathy factor going for him, and he did very well. I was third most effecttive: I had the gift of gab it took, but I didn't have the ploys that Jack and Johnny had. Dimpled-cheek, baby-face, butterball Jack was second best because he had the cute-factor going for him. Johnny got and sold the most because he had the pity-factor: shuffling with a gimp, affecting a partially paralyzed left arm, speaking with an impediment and drooling a little, he hit people smack in their tender mercies. (As for those who knew Johnny, the pity-factor turned into the comedy-factor: he couldn't lose.)

Most of the time scalping was straightforward fun and profit, but there were twists and turns. Say we had two tickets in different sections and a couple wanted two together. We would say the seats were together in hopes the couple wouldn't check. If they didn't check, tough: *caveat emptor*, let the buyer beware. If they did check, we'd say we had gotten them from someone who told us they were together and man oh man, had *we* gotten screwed!

There were other twists. Once a man told me his son was sick and couldn't make it to the game, and did I want a ticket to see the game or to sell? "Because you can have my son's ticket if you really want to see the game," he said. I assured him I wanted to see the game. "Well, come along then," he said. I explained I was supposed to meet a friend who hadn't showed up yet; when he arrived I'd tell him and then join the man in the stands. "Well, okay," he said, with a shade of doubt in his voice, and he handed me the ticket. My partner of the day, Jack, had a stack of tickets he was hawking, so I decided to sell this one myself. I held it up and called out, "I got a ticket here, who wants a ticket?" Suddenly a hand snatched the ticket and spun me around. It was the man. "You lied to me, you sonofabitch!" he hollered, then stalked off. I deduced a moral from this occasion: *Wait*.

One Saturday when T.U. was away, we went to an Oklahoma State game in Stillwater to ply our trade, but nobody had extra tickets. We were about to give up when a guy approached with several that he couldn't give us—they were simply too good, forty yard line no less—but he was willing to sell them at a good price. We bought them, but when we tried to sell them we quickly found out they were for the previous week's game. He'd got us good, but rather than feeling pissed off, we had a good laugh. Screwing, getting screwed, both were part of the game. And from this occasion we drew another moral: *read the fuckin' ticket*.

We scalped T.U. football games all three years we were in high school. While we were scalping, school chums would pass us by and look at us askance, kind of embarrassed that they knew these guys grubbing for tickets and hawking them like street peddlers. Johnny especially embarrassed them with his retard act. But what they didn't know, and what we weren't about to tell them, was that we averaged twenty-five, thirty bucks a game. In today's terms, at least two hundred dollars each.

## *An Initiation*

My sophomore year at Will Rogers—we had no freshman year—I played football on the B team, the junior varsity squad. The A squad players had an initiation ceremony of sorts—you could call it hazing—that they reserved for a few B squad players. I knew what it was because Don Brooks had told me about it.

After practice one day, a bunch of us B-squadders were in the shower room when two A squad players peeked around the doorway and scanned the room until they spotted me, then the lights went out. I knew I was "it." I was at the far end of the room, so I started sliding along the wall under the showers toward the door to make my escape. When the lights came back on the two guys were right in front of me. They laughed and grabbed me. I struggled, but suddenly there were two more grabbing me. They hauled me out of the room, kicking and writhing, where a couple more were waiting.

One had a wad of gauze in his hand, and on the gauze was a large dollop of what we called analgesic bomb, a liniment the consistency of Vaseline that smelled like root beer mixed with Absorbine Jr. You rubbed it into aches and pains, to give them the benefit of heat. Thus the name analgesic, I suppose, which means "without pain," only the word is a misnomer—at least it is when the goop is swabbed all over your ass and your crotch as all the players watching laugh and whoop and holler, and maybe that's why bomb was part of the name, because it felt like an explosion of fire burning my butt and my balls, and I knew that water wouldn't soothe it—in fact, water would only make it worse, by spreading the pain around—but that only time would take care of it, and quite a long time at that, like hours.

And yet, truth to tell—I daresay this will come as no surprise—I felt honored.

### *A Turning Point*

I started on the B squad football team at Will Rogers, then on the B squad basketball team as well. The basketball team was very competently coached by a quiet long-time staffer named Hogue who was assisted by an overweight, over-wrought, self-important young man from T.U. named Lane. All the other starters were guys I had played with before, some in grade school, some in junior high, some in both. I was the defensive specialist, the one they put on the other team's hot shot unless he was the center. I loved the role. To me, messing up another guy's game was at least as satisfying as scoring points.

Playing away was even better for basketball than football because we got to ride in the bus with the A squad. (Whereas the football teams had so many players that each squad had a bus of its own.) For some obscure reason, suiting up in a foreign locker room and playing on a foreign court before a foreign crowd made me feel like I was warming up for the Big Time, like running a play in Boston before heading to New York. Our fourth or fifth away game was in Bartlesville, prosperous company town of Philips Petroleum and an intense rival of Will Rogers.

The B squad played first. I was put on their main guard, a guy whose name I don't recollect but whose play I remember well. He was three or four inches taller than me and twice as quick. And he could hit shots from anywhere. If I guarded him against a long shot, he'd fake and zip past me for a layup or a hook. If I gave him some space to guard against a layup, he'd sink a jump shot. He was far better than anyone I'd ever played against, and I simply couldn't shut him down. But I did manage to foil him now and then, and I got some rebounds, assists, points. So did the rest of our team. We lost by two points, but given the difference in talent we should have lost by twenty. I thought so, at least.

In the locker room I got everyone to horsing around, flinging soap in each others' faces, snapping each other with towels, cracking jokes. Suddenly Coach Lane appeared. "All right, that's enough!" he bellowed. "Get dressed and get in the bus, now!" Silently we did as told and waited for him. In a few minutes he entered the bus and grimly stared at us, one by one. Then he said, "I have never seen such disgraceful behavior in all my life. Fooling around and laughing like that when you just lost a game! You know what they do at T.U. when they lose? They scream, they cry, they smash lockers! Cause they hate to lose!"

That was when I spoke up. "I don't like to lose, either, Coach, but I don't feel like cryin'. That was the best I've ever played in my life."

"But it wasn't good enough, was it, Duncan?"

"Not to win, but I'm willin' to practice twice as long and three times as hard to git better," I explained. "I just don't feel like cryin's all. That was the—"

"Yes, I know, the best you've ever played. So maybe you're just a loser, Duncan—have you ever thought o' that?" Then, looking from me to all the players, "Cause that's the bottom line, gentlemen: do you want to be a winner, or do you want to be a loser? The choice is yours. Think about it." Dramatically he paused again, looking us in the eye one by one, then made a huffy grand exit out of the bus.

We sat in silence for a bit, until someone said, "He's right." Then followed a chorus: "Yep. Right on the money. Losin's shit, man. Winnin's the name of the game. Damn right. Fuckin' A."

I didn't join the chorus. I didn't agree. Playing the way I did felt terrific, no matter the outcome. I would have felt better if we had won, sure, but that was no reason to feel bad. Only now I was feeling bad. For the first time in my life, I felt apart from the team I was on rather than a part of the team. Apart from old pals and teammates: Danny and Kenny, Jerry Don Garland, Mike Burton, Henry Hill.

As a consequence, I became acutely self-conscious, and my game fell apart. Dribbling when I should pass, passing when I should dribble, shooting when I shouldn't, not shooting when I should, cutting right when I should cut left and vice versa, passing to the wrong guy, passing to where the guy was rather than where he was going, missing passes thrown to me, missing shots, forgetting to follow up shots for the rebound, getting faked out by the guy I was guarding. Within two weeks I was on third string, where I stayed—*and belonged*—for the rest of the season. I was so down I didn't even try out for baseball.

Thus the high-school basketball and baseball careers I had anticipated for years came to an end, not with a bang, but a collapse. But come autumn, I said to myself, there would be football: I would redeem myself then.


### *Running Wild*

New Year's Eve my sophomore year Johnny, Jack, Rolly, and I got six six-packs of Jax—nine beers apiece— and retired to a vacant green house on Twenty-First Street where we sat in the tall dry brown grass and drank ourselves stupid—our first time—then staggered to the Delman Theater for the midnight show. We somehow got to the balcony where as soon as I sat down I passed out then woke up puking all over the girl in front of me. (Another relationship nipped in the bud.) I don't know how I got home. Next morning I was gravely hung over. Mom asked me how much I had drunk, then, after getting over her shock, told me I deserved all of my misery if not more. I didn't argue.

As for academics, here was the deal: It was always understood that I would go to college, but getting into one of the state universities was not that hard. From high school you just needed a minimum number of certain subjects—a couple years of science and math, three or four years of history and English, as I recall—and a C average. The difficulty was staying in college: the recruiting reps of both O.U. and O.S.U. boasted that their schools flunked forty percent of their freshmen, the point being their schools' academic rigor. (In Oklahoma back then, it seems, even college was a macho thing.) So I didn't feel any pressure to make good grades, and by God I didn't.

Geometry, for instance. In ninth grade I had passed algebra without understanding much of anything. In tenth grade I had the same two difficulties with geometry as I had had with algebra. The first was summoning sufficient interest to study it. Acute, isosceles, equilateral, trapezoidal, rhomboidal, hemorrhoidal, who gave a shit anyway? The second was understanding it when I did study. With algebra my problem was the letters that appeared in place of numbers, plus parentheses and italics and such; with geometry my problem was spatial relationships and configurations, plus parentheses and italics and such. In both cases my brain panicked, then shut down. The difference between the two classes was that the algebra teacher gave me a C I did not deserve, while the geometry teacher was going to give me the F I did. But to get into college I needed to pass. Just a D that I could balance off with a B in some other course. So at the term's end I offered the teacher a deal: in return for a D, I promised not to embarrass her by taking any more math classes. Otherwise, I pointed out, I'd have to take her class again. She gave me the D.

Sophomore English was another story. I couldn't stand the teacher. Miss Crate. She read aloud her favorite Romantic poetry, like Shelley feeling sorry for himself—"I fall upon the thorns of life, I bleed! I die, I faint, I fall!"—and Keats waxing ecstatic: "Oh, happy, happy boughs. Oh happy happy happy!" And Miss Crate reading this stuff with catches in her voice and tears running down her cheeks. In response to which I silently prayed for mercy and conspicuously did no work. Even slept through exams. And flunked the second semester. And didn't care, because I could take it again sometime.

But Mom did care. Sliding by was one thing, but getting an F was not sliding by. It was hitting bottom, coming to a stop. We argued and fought.

After basketball season I resumed drinking and, figuring one good vice deserved another, took up smoking. Johnny, Jack, and Rolly agreed. Billy, a superb wrestler, was another story: wild though he was, he wouldn't even drink pop, much less alcohol, much less smoke. But he loved to hang around with us guys who did.

It wasn't easy, learning how to smoke. Sucking that crud into your lungs and exhaling it in a casual sort of way, like Gene Kelly doing a little soft-shoe. Or talking with a fag dangling from your lips and pretending the smoke in your eyes didn't sting. And at first dealing with the dizziness and nausea, like running through the stitch in your side to get a second wind, only instead of getting wind we were fouling up lung. And we knew it. A common name for cigarettes was *coffin nails*, for God's sake. But smoking made us feel cool. It's a hell of a price to pay for cool, the money, the damage, but hey, no pain no gain: to us, cool was worth it.

It was ridiculously easy for a teenager to drink in Oklahoma back then because, paradoxically enough, it was a dry state. Or almost dry: three-two beer (i.e., beer with an alcohol content of three point two percent) was legal, but any and everything else wasn't and yet was readily available, even to minors. You wanted some whiskey, you bought it at a bootlegger joint—a hotel lobby, the backroom of a bar, etc.—or better yet, you called a bootlegger and it was delivered to your door, simple as that. Bootleggers were an integral and even a quasi-public part of life in Oklahoma. They couldn't join Southern Hills Country Club, but their kids could be a star athlete, president of the class, homecoming queen. Some bootleggers even passed out satirical business cards, like *Edwards' Home Furnishings: Jim Beam end table, $4.00; Jack Daniels davenport, $7.00; Johnny Walker love seat, $7.00; Cutty Sark dinette, $5.00.*

Since bootlegging was commonplace, corruption was commonplace, making the state a paradise for teens like my pals and me. We not only bought cigarettes and booze with no problem, we hung out in bars. The only time I was denied service was at the Elbow Room on Eleventh. For several weeks Rolly and I went there after school to recover from the strain of academic boredom with a beer or two, but then one afternoon the barmaid asked for our I.D.

"You know we're not old enough," I said. "Why're you askin' now?"

"Well, we got a new cop on the beat," she said. "Come back in a couple o' weeks."

Two weeks later we went back. "Done deal?" Rolly asked.

"Done deal," she said. "What'll you have?"

"The usual," we said, and the bar maid joined us as we toasted our good fortune to live in a time and place where the cops could be bought off so easily.

### Love Life

When puberty hit me broadside, Mom gave me a book about sex because she found the subject too embarrassing to talk about. It was written specifically for teenagers in a style about as arousing as the Boy Scout Manual. The facts, as Sergeant Joe Friday always said on *Dragnet*: just the facts. But I found certain facts—especially the ones about the vagina in a state of engorged and lubed excitation—as arousing as Johnny's dad's playing cards with the naked pinups that we lusted after as we jacked off, and I put the book to the same use, even though I knew damn well that that was not what Mom had in mind when she gave it to me.

One day Johnny told me someone had told him there was a way to masturbate that felt like actual screwing. What you did was, you got a loaf of Wonder Bread, cut a hole about two inches in diameter in one end, poured hot water through the hole until the bread was all hot and slippery-slick—one could almost say hot and bothered, Johnny said—then fuck it. So one day we did, him with his loaf, me with mine, and what I can tell you is, it worked, but it also made such a mess that we never did it again.

When we were twelve or so Johnny and I first heard about the Carolina Hotel, a whorehouse in a two-story brick building on First Street beside the Frisco railroad tracks, fairly close to downtown but off by itself, like a well-known pariah. The Carolina served not only as a resort for horny men, but also as a measure of local corruption: if we heard about it when we were barely pubescent, then you know damn well that every grownup in town who wasn't deaf and blind and senile knew about it as well, yet there it stood, doing a steady business unmolested by the law or the press night after night, year after year. The summer of fifty-five, despairing of getting laid by a girl in our peer group for free, Johnny and I went there one night to make our sexual debut.

We walked up an L-shaped staircase to a little lobby bare of furniture. Seven or eight young women in negligees came out of a room and lined up, a number of them surprisingly pretty—with looks like that, why were they whores in a two-bit hotel? Each of us picked one. They led us down a long corridor and into separate rooms. My girl asked me what I wanted. I thought it was a pretty dumb question—I wanted to get laid, obviously—but, seeing my hesitation, she elaborated: a quickie, a half-n-half, or an around-the-world. The first seemed self-explanatory, but I had no idea what the last two meant. I didn't want to betray my innocence, though, so I asked for a price list. A quickie, five bucks, she said; half-and-half, ten; around-the-world, twenty. My budget constrained me to a quickie, and my innocence betrayed my innocence: "You're a virgin, ain'tcha?" she remarked as I mounted, and quick it was. "Yep, a virgin alright," she said, smacking my bottom and pushing me off. It wasn't just quick, though; it was also rather flat, like stale beer, but afterwards I agreed with Johnny that it was fantastic—man oh man was it ever!—just as a few summers before I had agreed that boy-girl parties were the best.

Even though I was disappointed and even felt a little shitty afterwards, several weeks later I went back for more, with the same result: the expense of spirit in a waste of shame, as Shakespeare put it. And, as his poem goes on to say, a couple of months later, even though I knew what the outcome would be, I went back for more. Lust in action. But I judged that a whore was better than a girl friend. A whore was simple: you paid, you got laid, you got out of there, with none of the fuss and muss of a girl friend, even if she put out. So once in a while, when my hormones got to burning and churning, I dropped in at the Carolina to give them some relief. With all the smugness of sixteen, I reckoned I had my love life all figured out.

## *License*

I passed the driver's test right after my sixteenth birthday, and in return got a receipt, a small slip of paper with my name and address. It would serve as my license until the real thing came in the mail a few weeks later.

Less than a few weeks later Crowder and I were zipping down Fifteenth Street on his Harley late one Sunday night when, for the first time in three years, we got pulled over. Billy didn't have his license yet, so, congratulating myself on my guile, I whispered in his ear, "This doesn't have my description, so just say you're me," and slipped him my receipt as the cop walked up to us. A couple weeks after that I received a missive from the State of Oklahoma, but instead of the license I was looking for, it was a notification that lending a license to someone else was an offense punishable by a three-month suspension of said license forthwith, and that at the end of said three months I was to report to the Tulsa Youth Court for a hearing. So, before I even got the license that I had long been longing for, I lost it. But how, I wondered, could they know the license wasn't Billy's? That Billy wasn't me? That I wasn't him?

"Because you're much taller than Billy, and have red hair and green eyes while his hair and eyes are brown," Mom impatiently explained.

"But none of that stuff was on the license! It's not even a license! Just a receipt!"

"But all that stuff *is* on their records in Oklahoma City, Jeffrey!" she said in exasperation. "Otherwise, how could they put it on the license they were going to send you!"

"Oh," I said. So much for my guile.

"I know you're not stupid," she went on, "but I swear, sometimes you do things that are beyond stupid!"

"Yeah," I said, "I guess I do."

"I just hope and pray that someday you start to think," she said. "Wise up."

"Me too," I agreed, though I had no idea how long it was going to take before I did.

### *An Escapade in Pauls Valley*

The spring of my sophomore year we went to Pauls Valley for Easter—our last holiday there, because that summer Gram and Grad, disappointed that the reality of small-town life didn't live up to their memory or their dream, were moving to California. We took Billy with us. I had several acquaintances in Pauls Valley, and one good buddy, Larry Archer. Larry was one of nine kids whose father worked in some oil field nearby and whose mother heroically kept those kids, a wild bunch, in semi-check. I liked Larry a lot. Part Indian, tall and lean, black hair, dark skin, with a beak of a nose and a bit of an overbite, Larry was one terrific athlete who also had a sweet goofy streak.

The night before Easter, Billy and I went with Larry downtown to the pool hall where we met a few guys to shoot some breeze as well as some pool. I vaguely remember a nice guy named Herb Cathy, and distinctly remember a wild child appropriately yet improbably named Randy Rhoades. Randy told Billy and me that he liked to diddle calves and that we should try one sometime, because they were *good*, man, a damn sight better than commonly reputed—like for instance how one night he put it to this exceptionally pretty little calf, just as cute as a button and sweet as sugar cane, and how, just as he came, she shit all over him. Randy paused, then in a dramatic whisper he concluded, *"Boys, we had ourselves a goddamn mutual climax!"*

We shot pool and told more stories until we ran out of money, then wondered what to do. Wondered what we could do. There weren't a lot of options in such a small town. Randy suggested we gang-bang a calf, but, call us narrow-minded, unadventuresome fuddy-duddies, if you like, we all nixed the idea. Herb suggested Monopoly or Canasta, but we were too hopped up to sit around a table. Then Larry suggested we rob a bakery truck, explaining to Billy and me that there was this delivery guy who parked his truck in his front yard at night, and often left it unlocked, and sometimes there were leftovers—were we game? Is the Pope Catholic? we asked—just show us the truck.

We all piled in one car, six or seven of us, and drove by the guy's house, which was in the back of a deep lot. Sure enough, the truck was parked in the yard near the street, under a tree. We parked half a block away, crept up to the truck, and found the back doors unlocked. Larry and I crawled in and groped around in the dark until we felt cellophane-wrapped packages of various shapes and sizes. We tossed them to the others standing at the open doors. I even found a full-size pie. "That's enough," someone whispered, so Larry and I crawled back out of the truck. I carried the pie carefully—it was the holy grail of our haul.

We drove to a field at the edge of town. There, by the light of the silvery moon, we saw that we had scored big: cupcakes and cookies of various sorts, cream puffs, fried fruit pies, miniature pecan pies, cinnamon rolls, Danish pastries, plus the pie, a custard cream, it turned out. We gabbed and ate until we hit surfeit. We tossed the leftovers into the field, except the pie. Throwing that away would be a waste, a shame. But we were too full to eat it. What to do?

Then Randy said, "Man, I'd love to see this pie in Paul Allen's face," and the other PV boys yelled : "Oh man, that would be sweet! Serve that sonofabitch right! Motherfucker deserves it! Such an asshole!" I asked who Paul Allen was: Superintendent of Schools, they said.

"We'll do it," Billy said.

"But you guys'd get in a shitload of trouble," Larry said.

"No we won't," I said. "He doesn't know us from Adam. We're from out of town, man. Strangers. He'll never know who did it. How can he?"

"Are you guys sure you wanta do this?" Randy asked.

"Are you kiddin'?" Billy asked. "Throw a pie in a superintendent of schools' face!"

"If we passed up such an opportunity," I added, "we couldn't live with ourselves."

The PV boys cheered, and we piled into the car and took off. As we slowly drove by the Allens' house, we saw through the windows him and his wife in the living room, reading. We parked down the street and got out. I flipped a coin to see who got to throw the pie. Billy won. We all walked to the Allens' yard. The PV boys stopped at the edge, hiding behind bushes and trees, while Billy and I walked onto the porch. I opened the screen door and knocked. In a few seconds Allen opened the door and Billy pushed the pie into his face. Without a word Allen jumped back and slammed the door as Billy and I bolted off the porch and joined the others bustin' ass for the car. We piled in and drove off, the PV boys pounding Billy and me in a bellowing, guffawing fit of congratulation, admiration, and gratitude. The two of us glowed.

Next morning Gram, Grad, Mom, Billy, Chris, and I went to church. Afterwards we had Easter dinner, then Mom, Billy, Chris, and I drove back to Tulsa. I thought it was the last time I would visit Pauls Valley.

## Trouble, Trouble Everywhere

That spring, 1955, I wasn't playing baseball for the first time in years. Not surprisingly, I didn't fill that hole in my life by studying. Nor did I get a job. I still had the paper route, so I was making enough money to buy beer and to pay an occasional call on the Carolina. When I ran out of money I hung around the house fighting with Mom. She was not happy with me, but what could she do? Spank me? I could grab her arms and hold her still. Ground me? I had to leave the house, in the morning to deliver papers, and at night every week or so to collect. After collecting I'd hang out at a bar. When I ran out of money I'd stay home and fight with Mom.

So I was a major pain in the house, but by my reckoning at the time, Mom was the pain, always nagging me about this and that. Misbehaving in school (she got notes, phone calls). Not studying. Not playing ball. Sitting around doing nothing. Going out and drinking. Then I got a notice from the Police Department to appear in Youth Court in a couple weeks for a hearing about the loan of my license to Billy. He got one too.

Youth Court was where high school traffic offenders went for a hearing by their peers. The judge was a teenager. There was a cop supervisor, but he was there only to show that this was a real court. Instead of fines, the judge imposed essays of various lengths on traffic safety and so many weeks of traffic school depending on the gravity of the offense. I had never been to Youth Court, but everybody knew about it, it was such a fixture in Tulsa teenage life.

I was sick of sports, sick of school, sick of Mom and Chris, sick of Tulsa and its stupid police and Youth Court, and the real message of the state's notice, I decided, was to put all this shit behind me and start anew. In California, where Gram and Grad were moving. I could live with them. Gram understood me better than Mom did. And Aunt Jeanne and Uncle Earle were already there—I could move in with them until Gram and Grad arrived. And there were fabulous jobs out there: I could get one of some sort working outside year round in the California sun under palm trees with ocean waves crashing and splashing the beach nearby, and I could make really good money and screw gorgeous blondes with golden tans and big tits. I couldn't wait.

I gave the *World* my notice. Because we were to appear in Youth Court together, I told Billy of my plan (he said it sounded good: real good), but no one else. On the evening of our hearing I packed a small leather suitcase and dropped it out of my bedroom window on the side of the house where no one ever went. Wearing my blue suede jacket and my blue suede shoes, I told Mom and Chris I'd see them later, walked out the front door and around to the side, picked up my suitcase, and walked to the bus stop on Fifth Street where I met Billy.

We rode in silence to the bus station. Since I never saved money I didn't have much, so I figured I would take a bus west a ways, too far to be found, then hitchhike and work my way across the land doing odd jobs. The ramblin' man routine. I asked the ticket clerk for the cheapest one-way fare to a town, any town, in Texas. I specified Texas because that would mean I was really on my way, whereas a town in Oklahoma, even if it was clean over on the other side of the state, would have meant I had hardly left. She said Denison was the cheapest. I bought the ticket and told Billy I'd give him a call once I'd settled down in California. He said he'd be sure to come visit and walked out of the waiting room toward the nearby Police Station where Youth Court was held. I sat down on a pew-like bench to wait for departure.

The bus left around ten and arrived in Denison in the middle of the night. I had managed to sleep, but fitfully. From the bus station I walked down the street into a hotel lobby that looked like a set in a western: potted palms, brass spittoons, a large braided rug on the wood floor, globed glass lamps sitting on little round tables, stiffly upholstered sofas and chairs. I lay down on one of the sofas to get some more shuteye; no one bothered me.

I slept restlessly, then got up a few hours later, bought a doughnut and a cup of coffee, and walked along the main street, which was also the highway, through town. It was a sumptuous spring morning, sunny, balmy, soft, the kind that's so lovely it makes you yearn for something more even though you're euphoric with what you've got. I watched kids on their way to school, chatting, laughing, horsing around. Although I hadn't heard of him, I felt like Holden Caulfield, looking at that world of childhood I had left behind several years ago and could never go back to, but also feeling as though I had left it just last night—a heart attack of nostalgia.

I got a ride from someone I don't recall to Dallas. Dallas. You couldn't get any more Texas than that, so I felt I was well on my way. In Dallas I got a hamburger and then a ride from a good-sized dark-haired guy, thirty-five or so, in a white shirt with the sleeves rolled up to mid-forearm, a dark tie, and horn-rimmed glasses. Said he couldn't take me far, but he'd be happy to give me a ride as far as he could. We drove out of town into these rolling fields covered with bluebonnets. I could see why Texans made such a fuss over them: acres and acres of dense blue blossoms on green ocean-like swells, and the flowers and grass rippling gently in the breeze. Lovely.

This guy started asking questions. Where was I from? Oh, he'd been to Oklahoma, a lot. Always had a great time there. Great state. Great women. And where was I headed? California? Oh man, he loved California. Those Mexican girls. They get fat when they get older, but man oh man, when they're young, they are fine. Nice big tits. Nice plump asses, sweet pussies. Even when they're twelve, thirteen. He had this twelve-year-old Mexican girl once, with a body you wouldn't believe, set her down on his dick and popped her cherry—and she went wild. But hey, one time a buddy of his was riding the bus from Dallas to San Antone in the back seat, and there was this Mexican chick sitting beside him, just the two of them back there, and before they got to San Antone she gave him a blow job, right there on the bus! What did I think of that?

At first I wondered why this mid-thirties guy was talking so much sex to sixteen-year-old me, but now I was pretty sure why. I had encountered a queer (one of our two words for a gay man, the other being *fag*) only once before, when I was walking home one evening from a movie, and this tall slender young man asked me if I knew where he could find a whorehouse. I told him the Carolina Hotel. He asked if they gave blow jobs. Uncomfortable, I said I didn't know. He asked if I had ever had a blow job. Even more uncomfortable, I said no. He asked if I would like to have one. Angry now, I said no and started walking away. He said, "Why not, they're really good," but I said nothing, just kept walking, only by this time I was trembling and shaking with anger, and wishing I had a gun so I could shoot him.

Now, deep in the heart of Texas, I was playing for time because we were in the middle of blue-bonnet fields without a man-made structure in sight. If we could just get to a town or a village or a filling station. Or if I could please be wrong about this guy. But then he repeated the question: what did I think of that? I didn't want him to get the wrong idea, so, instead of playing for more time, I opted for bluntness. "I think your friend's fulla shit," I said.

"You think so?" he said. "Gee, I've always known him to be an honest guy."

"Yeah? Well, I think he's fulla shit."

Then came the clincher. "Have *you* ever had a blow job?" he asked.

Once again I was trembling inside in anger, but even more in fear—I mean, this guy was a man who was a good deal bigger than me—but his cards were on the table and I wanted no part of his game. So, feigning cool, I drawled, "Welllll, this is a purty good spot. You can let me out."

"Here?" he said. "In the middle of nowhere?"

"Yup," I said. "This is just about right."

"What's the matter?" he asked. "Did I say something wrong?"

Now I was terrified, because he hadn't started stopping, and he might be taking me wherever to do whatever, so I replaced cool with bluff: "Just let me out, you sonofabitch, or I'll kick your ass."

"Now hold on," he said. "I may let you out, but I don't know about any kickin' ass."

"If you don't stop this goddamn car you're gonna find out," I threatened, silently and desperately praying he didn't want to find out.

"Sure thing, pal, no sweat off my balls." He stopped and I got out with my little suitcase. He made a U turn and gunned it back toward Dallas. Yep, I thought: a fag alright. But I didn't feel like shooting him the way I did with the guy in Tulsa, just relieved.

It was really warm now, so I tied the sleeves of my blue suede jacket around my waist and stuck my thumb out. There weren't many cars, and they didn't even slow down. I didn't bother with trucks because I knew they weren't supposed to pick up hitchhikers. After a while I decided that getting somewhere, however slowly, was better than getting nowhere, so I started walking. When I heard a car coming I'd turn and make the sign, offering folks the chance to see my honest face, but, however honest-looking, my face didn't prove the least bit persuasive. They'd zoom by, I'd turn and walk until I heard another car coming, then turn and stick out my thumb until the car zoomed past, then turn and walk on admiring the bluebonnets, enjoying the sun and the breeze, and wondering what Mom was doing, Chris, my friends.

A semi passed me slowing down, then stopped on the shoulder. I ran up to it. The driver, grizzled, lean, and lanky, said he was going to Houston—would I like a ride? Houston. That was as Texas as Dallas. I said great and climbed in.

We got to talking. I told him about the queer I had just encountered. He told me a number of stories about folks he had run across with various and odd sexual druthers—

fetishists of all sorts (shoes, undies, silk scarves, fur coats, ear rings, wedding veils, douche bags), sadomasochists, piss and asphyxiation freaks—but he told them with lots of humor and without a hint of come-on. He wasn't interested in a romp with a teenager; he was just amused by the wacky ways some people have of getting off. He *was* interested in eating, though, as I found out when he pulled into a truck stop, explained he had spent all his money this trip getting two flats fixed, and would I mind buying him dinner? Well, I didn't have much, and he *was* exploiting me (now I knew why he picked me up), but he was also giving me a long lift, and he was keeping me good company in the bargain, so how could I say no?

He ate a big dinner. I ate a grilled cheese sandwich—the cheapest I could get—even though I was hungry as hell too, but I had to husband my meager resources. Which amounted to maybe two bucks when we left the truck stop and hit the road again. We talked all the way to Houston. He dropped me off in the outskirts, before he got to his terminal, since he wasn't supposed to pick up hitchhikers. I found myself in a neighborhood of salvage yards. Behind the salvage yards were woods, the trees exotically draped with Spanish moss. It was deep dusk. Not one person in sight, not one establishment open. I had nowhere to go, no one to see, nothing to do. I was tired, so I decided to turn in for the night. In the woods. The only place I could afford.

I put on my blue suede jacket and walked between a couple of salvage yards into the woods, where I immediately felt my feet sink a little. Swamp. Then I remembered hearing that Houston was built on a swamp. But hell, better soft swamp than hard rock, unless I got wet and caught my death. I groped my way deeper into the woods until I was beyond the glare of the street lights. Getting down on my knees and feeling around with my hands, I found a smooth spot that was a little damp, but not wet. I lay down, rested my head on my suitcase, lit a cigarette, and listened to the racket that the bugs and the frogs were making (nature at night is really loud down south). I wondered what everyone was doing back home. Mom. Chris. Gram and Grad. Billy. Johnny. Rolly. Jack. And then I wondered what I was doing here. What was I proving? That I could get by on my own? Oh, I was getting by alright, spending the night all by myself in a fucking swamp with two bucks in my pocket. And in a few hours I would have even less. Unless I gave up eating. This running away business was beginning to look pretty sorry. Pointless. Stupid. Still... From diving I had learned that when you start a dive don't stop—go all the way, follow through—or you're *sure* to smash. Yeah, but...

I decided to sleep on it.

Two or three hours later I woke up cold and very damp. I got up and, stiff as starch, sort of walked, sort of staggered like Frankenstein's monster into one of the salvage yards. I found an old Packard that was in pretty decent shape. I opened the back door and... I know this is going to sound like the proverbial lantern in the cave, but, honest to God, on the seat there was a blanket. I crawled in, closed the door, wrapped myself in the blanket, and went back to sleep.

But I didn't sleep well. When I woke up it was still dark. My body ached, my head ached, and my mouth tasted like an ashtray. An old Packard in a salvage yard was better than a swamp, but not by much. Not enough to stick this decision of mine out. Follow through, yeah—go all the way, you bet—but when you're diving head first into a deep pile of do-do and you don't have to, when you can crawl back out and start all over with family and friends and money and good food and a roof and a bed, well, I decided, sticking to a plan on principle, when the plan and the principle are both stupid, is even stupider. It was time to take Mom's advice, to wise up.

I walked back out to the highway, stuck out my hand, and immediately got a ride. The chain-smoking driver didn't talk much. He held his cigarettes right in the middle of his mouth; the smoke curled up into his eyes, but he didn't seem to mind. After about an hour he turned into another highway.

Since I was now headed for a specific destination instead of just vaguely west, I got out to hitch another ride.

Two or three rides later I was back in Dallas, in a neighborhood of nice but not ostentatious brick houses. A bit of breakfast had just about busted me, and I was hungry. It was time to put my ramblin'-man plan into action. I started knocking on doors. Those who answered looked at me warily. I must have been a bit suspicious looking: hair uncombed, face unshaved, eyes red with fatigue, blue suede jacket and jeans and blue suede shoes smeared with dried-out swamp mud, a little beat-up leather suitcase in my hand. I asked if they'd like me to mow their lawns. Without hesitation they said no. As I was walking up a sidewalk to yet another porch, a car pulled up and a man in a brown suit asked me what I was doing. I told him. He asked how old I was and where I was from. I told him. He asked what I was doing in Texas instead of being in school. I said I was touring. He told me to get in the car, that he was a cop and the next stop on my tour was the police station. I asked what for. Loitering, he said. I said I wasn't loitering, I was looking for work. He said if I didn't cooperate, he'd charge me with aggravated loitering. I said what's that? He said I didn't want to find out. I got in the car.

At the station he called Mom, explained the situation, asked if she could wire me ten bucks, said good, then put me on the phone with her. She asked if I was alright. I said I was, said I was sorry, said I was on my way back home. She said she was glad. I said I was too. She said she missed me. I said I missed her. We were both choked up.

It would be a couple of hours before the money arrived, and it seemed there were no crimes in progress that needed the cops' immediate attention, and they were curious about my short-lived odyssey, so we chatted. They asked where I had been headed, and when I told them California, they laughed and pointed out that if I had kept going the way I had been going, I would have wound up in the Gulf on a straight line to Vera Cruz. As in Mexico. Feeling more than a little stupid, I said that maybe I should get a compass, and they said that sometimes it does help to know the direction you're headed. We joked about my episodes with the queer and the truck driver and bantered about the Oklahoma-Texas rivalry until they told me where the Western Union office was and to take care of myself. I said I'd try.

At the office I had to wait another hour or two for the money. From Western Union I went to the bus station. A bus had departed for Tulsa only half an hour before; the next one didn't leave until midnight. Too late, I decided. I needed to clean up, to eat, to get some sleep. Next day I could take the bus as far as what was left of the ten would get me and hitchhike the rest of the way.

I got a room at the Y, took a long bath, and treated myself to dinner in the cafeteria. I had some time on my hands, so I decided to check out Dallas. Moseying along the sidewalks people-watching and window-shopping, I came across a little theater, the Fox, with posters of girls in various degrees of undress. I could not believe my luck. It was the very place Jack had recently told me about, a strip joint he had gone to when he was in Dallas where the girls performed all kinds of indecencies in the raw. And I had just happened on it!

I bought a ticket and went in. A few men were watching a movie of a girl stripping. I sat down, thinking the movie was a warm-up for the real live girls. When the girl on the screen finished her dance another came on. A man got up from his seat and sat next to me. He was breathing heavily. I still wasn't interested in getting a blow job from a guy, so I moved several rows and seats away. Another stripper did her bit on the screen, and then I realized that Jack had told me a whopper about a place neither he nor I had any idea I would ever come across, had lied just for the sake of getting me all excited about a pure (or impure, if you like) fiction. You sonofabitch, I laughed, and went back out to mosey around some more, until I came across a big theater that was showing a new movie I hadn't heard of and that hundreds of people had lined up to see. The posters looked interesting, so I got in line.

The movie was *East of Eden*. Being in such a roil myself, I completely identified with Cal's perplexity and passion, and with James Dean's intensity in playing that perplexity and passion, and with the intensity of the entire movie—it stirred me to the quick, down to my deep heart's core. Seeing *East of Eden* was another turning point in my life, though I didn't realize it at the time. I only knew that I wanted to see more movies with that kind of force and depth, and to read stories and novels the same.

Next morning I slept in late, got some coffee and a doughnut, went back to the bus station, and bought a ticket with the money I had left—just enough to get me to Crowder, Oklahoma, which struck me not just as ironic, but also as significantly coincidental: the very same name as Billy's! What exactly the coincidence signified I couldn't say, but it seemed to promise some sort of improvement in my fortunes. I wondered how Billy had fared in Youth Court. On the wall map, Crowder was a spot right outside of McAlester, only ninety miles or so from Tulsa. I could easily hitchhike the rest of the way.

In the middle of the afternoon the driver dropped me off at the Crowder bus station, which happened to double as a Texaco station. Small town, Crowder. I watched the bus drive off, then posted myself on the highway and stuck my hand out when cars approached. After an hour I also stuck it out when trucks approached. No luck. After two hours I went into the station and spent almost all the money I had left on a Pepsi. The attendant, a skinny guy about thirty with a wad of tobacco in his cheek, looked at me as if I were a little odd, but said nothing. I started to leave and he said, "You cain't take that Pepsi out less you pay the deposit."

"You're kiddin'," I said.

"You wish," he said.

"I'm not gonna steal it," I said.

"You leave, you pay. Comp'ny policy."

*Nit-pickin' hick*, I thought to myself, and gave him two cents, stepped outside, drank my pop, set the bottle down, and went back out to the highway. I tried my luck until it was almost dark. No one even slowed down. I couldn't figure out why. I went back into the station.

"How the hell can a guy get a lift around here?" I asked.

"Probly cain't," he said.

"Can't? Why not?"

"Probly count of all the signs warnin' everbody not to pick up hitchhikers."

"You mean, there are... But why?" I asked.

"Cause they might be excaped pris'ners, like all the warnin' signs say," he explained, and immediately I smacked myself in the forehead with dismay. McAlester was the site of the state pen! And I *knew* it! I had just for*got*! Jesus, *would I ever learn!*

But to save some face—if only a very little—I said, "I'm not from around these parts. Why didn't you tell me?"

"I figgered you could read."

There was only one thing left to do. I asked if there was a phone. He pointed to a booth at the edge of the driveway. I dug a nickel and four pennies out of my pocket and asked for a dime. He said he wasn't running a charity. I went out to the driveway to see if I could find a coin, then spotted my empty Pepsi bottle next to the wall. I took it inside and asked for the two-cent deposit. He said I hadn't paid for it, but when I reminded him that he wouldn't let me take it outside without paying for it, he gave in.

I called Mom, collect. When I finished explaining my self-induced predicament, all she could say was, "Oh Jeffrey, Jeffrey, Jeffrey, Jeffrey, Jeffrey." And all I could say was, "I know, Mom, I know, I know, I know, I know, I know."

Finally she said to stay there, someone would come fetch me. I sat on the warm pavement, my back against the building, for two hours, swatting away gnats and watching June bugs crawl around on the screen door and moths bat around in the lights over the gas pumps, and mulling over the depressing fact that not only had I failed to get to California—had in fact been going the wrong damn direction!—I couldn't even manage to get my dumb ass back to Tulsa.

A good friend of ours, Brant Miller, pulled into the station. Brant worked for some oil company or other. He was married to a very bright, very funny woman named Evelyn who drank too much. They had a son Chris's age—Allen—and a younger daughter, Cheryl. Brant often took his kids and Chris and me, and sometimes Mom as well, to Fort Gibson Lake to go fishing and water-skiing. Evelyn didn't go much because she didn't enjoy the great outdoors. Mom didn't ski, and she only pretended to fish—the only time she got a bite the fish pulled her unattended pole into the water—but she liked to take a break from all her work at home and at work.

Occasionally Brant rented a cabin and we'd spend the weekend, and then Evelyn would come along. I always felt better then, partly because I liked her—I have always been partial to fun-loving drunks—and partly because when she wasn't with us, Mom and Brant seemed like a couple, and while that didn't feel wrong exactly, it didn't feel exactly right, either. The way they got along, I suspected an attraction, even though they never touched. (Later, after Mom died, her brother, my Uncle Bob, told me they *were* in love with each other, for years, but never let their relationship turn into an affair.)

Mom wanted Brant to be a father-figure for Chris and me, and no wonder—former football player at O.U., successful businessman, good father, generous spirit. Moreover, for Mom's sake, and probably for ours as well, Brant was willing to take on that role. So it made sense that he would be the one to drive ninety miles to pick me up in the middle of the night in the middle of the week—it was just the job for a father-figure.

He told me to get in. I put my suitcase in the back

seat, got in the front, and said, "Thanks for comin' to git me." Without replying, he took off.

We didn't say anything for quite a while. I felt too foolish, too indebted, too awkward to start a conversation, and I guessed he felt too angry, put-out. But finally he said, "I just want you to know that I came to get you because your mother's too tired and upset to do it herself. You've worn her to a frazzle, son."

"I'm sorry."

"You oughta be. Your mother's a great lady. Working full time, maintaining a home, raising you and Chris. Raising kids is a tough job married, but alone, single...?"

"Yes, sir. I know."

"Actually, son, you don't know. But maybe some day you will."

"Yes, sir."

"So why'd you take off anyway? The trouble in Pauls Valley?"

"What trouble?"

"C'mon. You and Billy throwin' a pie in the superintendent of schools' face."

"How do you know that? We didn't git in trouble for it."

"Oh? The day after you took off, two cops drove all the way from Pauls Valley to arrest you and Billy. They took him back to Pauls Valley and threw him in jail, and there's a warrant out for your arrest."

"But how could they know we did it? We're from out of town."

"My God, son, how stupid can...? It's a *small town*! You two stuck out like buck teeth! *Everyone* noticed you!"

"But how'd they know it was us that threw the pie?"

"I suspect because at least one of your partners in crime snitched on you. At least one always does. Don't you know that?"

I felt the same as when Mom explained how the cops knew my license receipt wasn't Billy's, as when I was told that Dallas was south of Tulsa instead of west, as when I learned that the town of Crowder was next door to the state pen. Because it was all so obvious. Of course everyone knew who we were. I was the grandson of J. B. Kellogg, public accountant, member of the Lions Club, the Chamber of Commerce, the First Methodist Church. And of course someone snitched, to save his ass. I felt not just ignorant, not just stupid, but downright imbecilic.

"What're they charging us with?"

"The talk is trespassing. Assault and battery. Malicious destruction of property."

"For throwin' a pie in a guy's face?"

"Not just a guy, son. The Superintendent of Schools. You've even made the newspapers. Tulsa as well as Pauls Valley. Front page. And you know, I was working on getting a scholarship for you. At T.U. But with your grades, and now this, there's no way."

"I didn't know," I said. "I'm sorry."

"So am I," Brant said. "And so's your mom."

We drove the rest of the way in silence. Brant had said what he had to say, I assumed, and he wasn't in the mood for chitchat.

When we got to the house, I found not only Mom and Chris waiting for me, but Gram and Grad as well. They all welcomed me with hugs and, on the part of Mom and Gram, some tears and kisses. It felt good, really good, to be welcomed with open arms.

They wanted to hear the story of my trip. I told them a bowdlerized version, which they found amusing, then Grad asked me if I would go with him and Gram to Pauls Valley the next day and turn myself in, to save the cops there the trouble of coming to get me here. It would be the diplomatic thing to do, he said. Surprised that he asked, and quite happy to take advice and try diplomacy for a change, I said yes.

On the way to Pauls Valley Grad said he knew Paul Allen from civic affairs and would really appreciate it if, in addition to turning myself in, I would apologize to the man. I said I couldn't apologize honestly: I was sorry for all the trouble I had caused the family, truly, but not about the pie in the face. And Grad—who at times could be irascible, arbitrary, demanding, and petty, but who in a pinch was always absolutely there for you—Grad said, "Alright. If that's the way you feel, that's all there is to it." And it was—he didn't ask me to apologize again.

In Pauls Valley we went to the court house, where Grad introduced me to the D.A., I guess he was, and I turned myself in. "Looks like you boys took a little more out of that bakery truck than you could chew," he said.

I was surprised he knew about that, but still managed to innocently ask, "Bakery truck? What bakery truck?"

"The one that donated the pie," he said. "I could charge yall for theft, but leavin' that truck unattended and unlocked?... I guess I could charge Jamie for possessin' an attractive nuisance, couldn't I?"

"It sure attracted me," I confessed.

"And it's proving to be a helluva nuisance," Grad quipped.

"There you go," the D.A. said: "My point precisely."

I signed some forms, Grad wrote a check for bond so I wouldn't have to go to jail, the D.A. said there would be a hearing sometime or other and told me to take care of myself. Grad and I went home to have lunch with Gram, then we all drove back to Tulsa.

When I returned to school on Monday, a week and two days after I had last attended—a stretch of time that seemed like a month if not longer—I got a note toward the end of the day to see Vice-Principal Hipsher, the man in charge of discipline. Warren Hipsher and I were well-acquainted because I got sent to him with a considerable degree of regularity. Rather tall and lean, with black hair, an awkward splay-footed gait, and a down-home drawl, he was funny but straight—no B.S. I liked the man. And he liked me, mainly because, I think, I never tried to B.S. him. If I had made the trouble I was sent to him for, I said so. So that, on the rare occasion when I hadn't, he believed me.

"I understand you've been doin' some travelin'," he said to me for openers.

"I thought I'd check out Texas," I answered.

"And?"

"The bluebonnets are beautiful."

"That's what I hear. You thinkin' o' doin' us all a favor and movin' there?"

"No, sir. Don't git me wrong—it's nice—but there's no place like home."

"It's nice to be wanted, is that it? Even when it's the law that wants you?"

"Oh, home's Tulsa. I'm just wanted in Pauls Valley. And I turned myself in already."

"So what happens now?"

"I don't know. I guess there'll be a trial or sumpn."

"It's that sumpn I want to talk to you about, Jeffrey. A lotta people here are wonderin' who it is the Pauls Valley boys are gonna nail."

"Pardon?"

"C'mon, Jeffrey—don't play innocent with me. Billy told the reporters your deal was tit for tat. It was in the *World* AND the *Tribune*."

"So *that's* why all my teachers have been so nice to me today!"

"Why, you don't suppose it's because they like you, do you? So who's it to be, Jeffrey?"

"We never made a deal like that, Mr. Hipsher. Billy must've been puttin' 'em on."

"You levelin' with me? No bull?"

"I swear. As a matter of fact, I'm sort of embarrassed we didn't think of it."

He looked at me for a moment, then said, "I bet you are. Well, let me just say, if someone here does get something like a pie in the face, you'll be expelled for good. Then you'll have to move if you want to finish school. You know that, don't you?"

"Yes sir."

"Good. Now stay out of any more trouble and spare me the pleasure of your company, will you?"

"Yes sir." He looked down at some papers on his desk, and I asked, "Aren't you gonna suspend me?"

"So you can miss another week o' school? You must be kiddin'! Now go on back to class and behave yourself."

"Yes sir," I said, and I did, because, 1) there wasn't much term left, and 2) if I didn't behave, Hipsher would expel me and Mom would probably kick me out of the house and I would be on my own, and 3) after my little Texas jaunt I didn't care to try that again.

The next day during study hall the teacher in charge, Bobby Goad, called me to his desk. Goad was the head varsity football coach. He was a tall, lean, soft-spoken man with high cheek-bones, a stereotypical Indian nose, a wide narrow-lipped mouth, and a mean glint in his eye. As I stood at his desk he looked me up and down, then said, very quietly, "You may think you're pretty cute, Duncan, throwin' a pie in a superintendent of schools' face, but I don't. So just in case you're plannin' on comin' out for football, don't bother. We don't want punks, and you are a punk. A chickenshit punk. Now go back to your seat and pray that someday you'll be a man."

"Yes sir," I said. I went back to my seat feeling hot and heart-sore and numb all at the same time. I'd never been kicked off a team before, much less before I had even gone out for it, and I'd never been called a punk by a coach, so his words hurt. Bad.

Several days later Gram and Grad drove to Tulsa again for a visit. Grad told us that Paul Allen had filed charges—trespassing, assault and battery, malicious destruction of property, just as Brant had said—but only against Billy and me, none at all against any Pauls Valley boys. Grad was furious. Said that Allen was currying favor with the locals because he wasn't the most popular guy in town. And the charges were way out of line with the deed itself, making a custard pie in the face into a felony. "I'm glad you didn't apologize to the sonofabitch," he told me.

A day or so later Billy and I got a bill from an insurance company for the damage to the Allens' hardwood floor, rug, couch, chairs, and drapes—eight hundred dollars. In today's terms, at least twenty-five hundred each. "The bastard must have smeared it all over the living room," Grad fumed. "Looks like he wants you and Billy to pay for refurnishing his house. Well, up his." I asked what I should do about the bill. "Don't do anything," he said. "*He* did the damage, let *him* pay for it." I asked about court proceedings. "Don't worry about it," he said: "we'll get a lawyer and get the charges reduced to something reasonable. I mean, you and Billy did wrong, and you should pay for it, but felonious assault? Malicious destruction of property? Hogwash!"

Well, Grad said don't worry, so I didn't. Weeks went by, then Allen got caught superintending one of his teachers in the sack. He fled town with her, and that was the end of this story. In terms of final consequences, I got kicked off a team before I even got on it, but that was all; there were no more notices from the insurance company, no hearing or trial, no jail, no fines, no citizenship classes, no rehabilitation essays, no community service, no penalty of any sort—an anti-climactic conclusion in which Billy and I did *not,* if you'll pardon the expression, get our just desserts, thanks be to God perhaps and to Paul Allen's libido for sure.


### *Uh Oh*

When I got my license back, Mom let me use the car—a forty-six two-door fast-back Pontiac—but with a restriction. She didn't drive it to work, so I needn't drive it to school, which was only a few blocks away. But she left the house before I did, and I was often running late, and I got home before she did, so how could I get caught? And I liked to go off campus for lunch, and the nearest hamburger joints were on Eleventh, half a mile away, too far to walk there, eat, and walk back in time for class. So I took the car.

One morning I was running late because I was watching the *Today Show*. I liked the host, the tall, easy-going, glasses- and bowtie-wearing Dave Garroway, and his sidekick, the little chimp J. Fred Muggs. The two of them were sort of an intellectual version of Tarzan and Cheetah. On this particular day Dave was interviewing a psychologist who had just published a book on teenagers, so they were talking about how my peers and I were idealistic, optimistic, energetic, etc., but also self-centered, impulsive, insecure, thoughtless, reckless, maniacal, disrespectful, intolerant, etc., and as the psychologist made each point I found myself laughing and muttering, "Yep, that's me alright." At the end of the interview Dave asked the man how he came by his love of teenagers, and he said, "Love? I don't love 'em. They're a remarkably unlovable, obnoxious group of people. But I do find them incredibly interesting." I cracked up, then recklessly drove like an interesting, obnoxious maniac to school.

Come lunch time I was hustling down the stairs from the top floor and saw through a large window a fire truck in the parking lot, the truck surrounded by a bunch of students. My heart went out to the poor bastard who needed the services of a fire truck. When I looked out the window on the next floor, I realized that the fire truck was parked in the general vicinity of my car. On the next floor, the first, I could see that it was parked much closer to my car than I had realized on the second floor and I began to think, "Oh no. Oh please God no." By the time I got to the edge of the lot I could see it was right next to my car—my car, did I say? *Mom's* car!—and I was running and moaning, "Oh shit, oh shit, oh shit oh shit." Two firemen had just finished putting out the fire. The charred rear seat and rearback were lying on the pavement. The rear windows were smoked, and the headliner was hanging in shreds like black Spanish moss. The front seats were not damaged, amazingly, but the entire car, inside and out, was drenched.

"This your car?" one of the fireman asked me.

"Yes sir."

"You're lucky we got here in time. It could've blown up, done a shit load of damage. You have any idea how it could've happened? You smell anything drivin' this morning?"

"No sir."

"You smoke? Your buddies smoke?"

"Do dogs bark?" a student quipped.

"Is water wet?" said another.

"You drink?" the fireman asked. "Your buddies drink?"

"Do birds fly?" another student observed.

"Do buffalo roam?" quipped yet another.

"Would yall shut up?" the fireman said, then turned to me. "You drive the car recently with some of your buddies, havin' a good time?"

"This past weekend, yes sir."

"Then this is what I suspect happened: one of 'em dropped a lit cigarette in the back seat, and it's been smolderin' for several days, but slow enough you didn't notice, and today it finally got hot enough for the seat to ignite."

"Well," I said, "thanks for puttin' it out."

"All in a day's work," the fireman said, then he joined his partner in putting their gear away as the students began favoring me with commentary: "I knew your car was hot, Jeff, but not this hot! I wonder how you're gonna explain this. Maybe you could say the commies torched it. How about spontaneous combustion? God almighty, it smells like soggy burned toast. I guess this just isn't your day." And so on.

About the time Mom usually got home from work— the moment I was dreading—I heard her shriek, then shout, "Jeffrey Light!" I stepped outside. She was staring at her burned-out sopping-wet Pontiac in the driveway. "What in God's name have you done this time?" I told her the truth and nothing but the truth, partly because I felt I deserved whatever was coming to me, and partly because I couldn't think of a story that would begin to hold water. When I finished my tale of disobedience, folly, and woe, Mom said, "Well, whatever this costs beyond our deductible, Jeffrey, *you* are going to pay the difference."

As it turned out, I had to lay out about two hundred bucks, but we got new windows, a new headliner, new rear seat and rearback, new seat covers, new door panels, new carpeting—a whole new interior. Even so, the car smelled like wet burned toast for months.

I didn't get to drive it again until September.

### Working Hard, Hardly Working

The summer of fifty-five Mom asked Richard Dickason, an old childhood friend of hers who was a contractor, if he could give me a job. Not only did he say sure thing, the next day he drove me across the Arkansas River to a site he was developing, over in West Tulsa. Along the way he told me about college, as Mom had asked him to, but not exactly as she had asked him to: what he did, he said, was wrestle, and what he learned—all he learned—was how to wrestle better. The development was a huge Levittown kind of project—two and three bedroom wood-frame houses with one bath and a dining area instead of a dining room and no trees whatsoever. Richard introduced me to a foreman, told me to do whatever the foreman told me to do, wished me well, and drove off. The foreman looked me over, scowled and scratched his head, then said to himself, "Oh what the hell," and took me to one of the crews and told them to find something for me to do. Obviously my job was a gift, not a necessity, and since Richard was a friend of Mom's from way back, I determined to hustle, to work hard and earn this job.

The men used me as their gofer: I got tools and lumber for them, carried buckets of water and bags of sand and concrete, dug trenches to lay in footings, fetched food and pop and cigarettes from a concession truck, whatever they wanted. We finished at three, and the foreman told me to be back at starting time, six o'clock. Six to three—a schedule dictated by the summer heat.

One of the crew was a lanky, thirty-ish, good-natured guy named Roger who lived near me. He took me home and agreed to pick me up in the mornings and take me home in the afternoons. In his pickup Roger and I listened to country music, drank coffee, smoked cigarettes, and joked about working and smoking ourselves to death. After several days the boss figured out a real job for me—to level out the ground within the foundations in accordance with Federal Housing Administration specifications. (There were no basements; I don't know why, but very few houses in Oklahoma have basements, even though it's the tornado capitol of the universe.) Since it looked like there were more houses than I could ever do, and since I didn't like working alone, and since Jack and Johnny wanted a job, I asked the foreman if he would hire them, and he said yes.

Next morning they met at my house for the ride with Roger. For the next few weeks, going to and fro, the four of us drank coffee and pop and smoked and listened to country music and sometimes sang along, and made jokes not only about working and smoking ourselves to death, but also about honkey-tonking and drinking and screwing ourselves to death, and if we didn't die, then jacking off into hairy-handed blindness and insanity. Roger enjoyed being a teenager again.

Another teenager joined us, Ronnie, who had some connection other than mine. Ronnie was blonde, slender, and delicate. He wore gloves to protect his hands; we worked barehanded, to get calluses, proofs of our toughness. He wore a straw hat to guard against the sun, and the hat was round-brimmed, like a woman's; we went hatless, to get burned and tanned, to show we did manly work out of doors.

Ronnie rested a lot, leaning on his shovel and wiping his brow with a bandana; we worked fast and stopped as seldom as possible, to prove how strong we were.

But then Jack took to leaning on his shovel and wiping his brow, and soon was complaining about back pain. In a couple of weeks we finished leveling the dirt within the houseless foundations, so the boss told us to level the dirt under houses—i.e., to crawl under and work sitting or squatting or lying down. We quickly found that when all four of us worked under a house at the same time we just got in each other's way, so we paired off. Johnny and I tried working with Jack and Ronnie, but they irritated us they did so little, so we stuck with each other and made them keep each other company, as we put it. But this arrangement irritated us as well—they often just sat under a house and gabbed, doing nothing but keeping each other company. It wasn't fair, all of us getting paid the same, but them doing next to nothing while John and I were busting ass, so we railed at them. Ronnie said his hands hurt, Jack said his back hurt. We snorted and scoffed.

"Go ahead, laugh, butthooks," Jack said, "but no one can see us underneath the houses, and if we work like fuckin' maniacs, we'll finish and be out of a job. Wise up, for God's sake."

"We're gittin' paid to work, you lazy sonofabitch," Johnny said, and I added,

"Not sit around shootin' the shit!"

"If yall wanta work so bad, then work, goddamnit! We're not stoppin' ya!"

Unable to think of a reasonable rejoinder, we said, "Aw, fuck you," then didn't speak to Jack for weeks, nor he to us. Johnny and I found it surprising that Jack had such a lazy streak, and, just as surprising, that we had such a self-righteous one.

In a couple of weeks we ran out of foundations to level, and on a morning so fine you wanted to drink it, the foreman let us go. Jack turned to Johnny and me and said,

"Thanks a lot, buttwipes." Hitchhiking home together, Johnny and I wondered how a guy who was so wrong could be so right.

### *Filling Station Blues*

After the construction job dried up, Johnny got a job at a Hudson's Gas Station on East Eleventh near the Will Rogers Theater. A few days later his manager told John that the Hudson station over in West Tulsa needed a hand, and John told me to go see the manager there, a guy named Cleo. I immediately took a bus downtown, transferred, rode out across the Arkansas to the Hudson station on West Eleventh (of course), and introduced myself to Cleo, a trim little man about thirty with tattoos on his arms, a matchstick in his mouth, and an edge in his voice. Yeah, he needed a hand, did I know anything about fillin'-station work? No, sir, I said, but I'm willin' to learn. Would I mind workin' till closin' time, eleven, and startin' in the morning at eleven? That would be fine. He looked me over warily. Would I mind gittin' dirty? No. Would I mind startin' now? I was hopin' to. Would seventy-five cents an hour suit me? I was hopin' for a dollar. Did I want the job or not? I wanted the job and went to work.

It wasn't convenient working there, because the bus took an hour each way. I got home around midnight, and next morning I had to catch the ten o'clock bus, so while I could get the sleep I needed, I had no time for anything else. One night, though, I went out until the bar closed at two and, predictably, next morning I overslept. There was no way I could get to work on time by bus, so I called Billy to see if he could give me a ride. He said sure.

At the time Billy was driving a forty-one Nash, a car that looked like an upside down bathtub on wheels. For years it had sat rusting in the grass between the corrugated metal shop and the stock tank, composing a scene that looked like a cartoon of hillbilly culture. Billy's dad agreed to let him drive the car if he could get it running. Billy worked on it for a week and got it running, but barely: it had very little power, and every day it seemed to have less. It also started smoking, and as its power decreased, its smoke increased.

The Nash did okay that summer morning—i.e., it moved us toward our destination—until we came to a rise (hill would be a gross exaggeration). Billy took off from the light, shifted to second, then to third, then the car started slowing down and smoking, so he downshifted to second. When he popped the clutch the motor roared, but instead of a surge the car kept slowing down and blowing more smoke, so much that it began filtering up through the floorboards. At about five miles an hour Billy yanked the gear shift into first. The motor roared even louder but the car kept slowing down as the black smoke from the exhaust now poured through the floorboards so thickly we could no longer see and could barely breathe. And then we felt the car come to a stop. And then we felt it start rolling backwards, back down the street with the gear in first and the motor roaring full-bore and smoking like an oil-well fire. Billy turned the wheel and somehow backed into a side street. We got out sputtering and laughing and rubbing our eyes, then pushed the car next to the curb. "Well, thanks for the ride, man," I said, and he replied, "Any time, pal." I took a bus one way, Billy took one the other and left the Nash to its fate: probably a tow to a salvage yard. I never saw it again.

Cleo wasn't amused at my reason for being late. Cleo never found me amusing. Everything I did aggravated him. I didn't know dick about how to talk to customers, how to clean windshields, how to pump gas, to check and add oil, to inflate tires, to take payments, to make change, to sweep the garage and driveway, to clean the bathrooms, to empty the trash. Several other guys worked there as well, and for their edification and delight Cleo constantly made quips at my expense. I wondered why he didn't fire me, then finally got it: putting me down lifted him up.

Then I discovered that Cleo was more (or less, actually) than just a small-time bully. I saw his wife a couple of times—she was young, pretty, sweet, and very pregnant. A couple weeks later Cleo gave me a cigar—she had had the baby the night before, he explained, a girl. He and the other two guys there were hung over, but they were also feeling pretty smug, with many a nod, a wink, a nudge, a snicker. After Cleo left for the day, Chuck, a twenty-ish tow-head who always wore red and black cowboy boots, couldn't contain himself and told me the story. After his wife had delivered, Cleo took the two of them out honkey-tonkin', first to some bars where they got ripped, then to a whorehouse where they got sucked and fucked, treats all on Cleo. What a night. Hooeey.

After that I didn't care what Cleo thought of me. I knew what I thought of him. Not that I was above low-life—I liked down and dirty—but not *that* down, not *that* dirty.

A few days later a customer came in one night asking for an oil change. Since I had never even heard the phrase, I had no idea what he meant. I couldn't ask the other guy on the night shift, Ernie, a skinny fellow nearing middle-age with large tobacco-stained teeth, because he had told me never to interrupt him when he was serving a customer, so I told the man I didn't do oil changes. In a pique of disbelief he drove out of the station peeling rubber. After Ernie finished his customer, he asked me what had happened. I told him. "So why didn't you change his awl!"

"Change it into what?" I asked. "Gas? Water? Kool-Aid?"

He stared at me a second, then said, "You don't know what an awl change is, do you?"

"I guess not," I said, frustrated, wondering how in hell I was supposed to know something I had never heard of, so I added, "There's a whole slew o' things I don't know—how about you?"

Ernie stared at me some more, then spit a big dollop of tobacco juice into a trash can and said, "Jesus Christ, you *are* stupid."

Next day he told Cleo. I guess picking on me had lost its many charms because, after declaring in a stern but gleeful huff that the business couldn't survive such an idiot as me, Cleo gave me the boot. Which was fine by me—I was about to quit anyway.

(Afterword: Three months later I found out how Cleo could afford to treat himself and the boys to honky-tonks and whores—he got caught treating himself to the Hudson till and wound up doing time.)

### *To Noel and Back*

Late one bright and beautiful Saturday morning, a week after I had been fired, Billy called and hollered, "Let's go to Noel!" I asked how, and he said, "How the hell you think? In my car! Call Jack and John. I'll put together what we need and be at your place pronto!" He hung up.

After the Nash expired, Billy bought a thirty-eight Chevy coupe—a two-seater with a large trunk. He had designs on it, to turn it into a hotrod, but as of yet the only thing he had done was cosmetic, getting it painted turquoise. Noel was (and still is) a little resort town on the Elk River in the Missouri Ozarks, about a hundred miles from Tulsa. Great water- and girl-sport in Noel, we had always heard: camping, swimming, diving, bag-swinging, tubing, canoeing, plus drinking, and dancing with your pick of gorgeous girls who were game for bedtime sports as well.

Johnny and Jack's folks gave them a lift to my house where we waited for Billy, but not for long. He pulled up honking the horn, gunning the engine, and hollering, "Let's go, goddamnit, hustle, let's git goin'!" He had fastened the metal arms of the trunk to hold the lid wide open. On the floor of the trunk he had spread blankets. On each side of the trunk were sleeping bags and a couple of bags full of groceries. "Jeff, you and Johnny ride in the trunk. Jack, you ride up front with me." The three of us took our assigned positions. Mom wished us luck, adding we would probably need it, and we were off.

Facing back with our feet on the bumper and no glass between us and the air, watching the road and countryside recede as we barreled ahead seventy-five miles an hour, speculating on the aquatic and amorous adventures that lay ahead, Johnny and I found riding in the trunk a real pleasure.

We stopped in Grove, a little town on Grand Lake where Jack had told us about a high-riding dock with a fantastic bag swing, a forty foot rope hanging from a tower as big as an oil derrick that leaned out from the dock at a forty-five degree angle. You could swing so high that when you let go you could do a double flip easy, he said. Well, there was a derrick-like tower, alright, but it was maybe seven feet high, and it stuck straight up at the edge of the dock which was three feet above the water. Which meant that the rope was only about seven feet long, which meant in turn that right after you jumped you had to release otherwise you landed right back where you started from just like that. No wonder we had the place all to ourselves: it was the worst bag swing we had ever seen. Jack laughed. Billy, Johnny, and I threw him into the lake with his clothes on. Then we all put on our bathing suits and dove in—a little disappointment wasn't going to spoil our fun.

After a while, as the afternoon began to slip into something cooler and more comfortable—namely, evening—Billy hollered, "Let's eat!" We followed him to his car. From the bags he pulled out a loaf of bread, a jar of peanut butter, a jar of jelly, a couple cans of pork and beans, some plastic knives and forks, and a can opener. Jack asked if this was dinner, and Billy said, "You don't like it, fat-ass, don't eat it." We made sandwiches, ate out of the cans, turned dinner into a food fight, cleaned up, and got back in the car.

"Get out, you guys," Billy said, "and give me a push." We asked him what was the deal. He said, "The starter don't work." We asked why he hadn't fixed it or got a new one before suggesting this trip. He said, "Why should I? I got you guys." We asked why *he* didn't push. "Cause I'm the driver and it's my fuckin' car! So push, goddamnit!"

It was almost dark as Johnny and I lay in the trunk talking about life when suddenly the car lurched with a god-awful screeching roar. We sat up to see millions of sparks shooting back into the darkness as the car slowed down and the sparks abated until we came to a stop on the shoulder in utter silence—even the bugs were stunned by the commotion, it seemed. We all got out saying, "What the hell...," walked around the car and found the problem. The right front wheel had fallen off. The whole thing. Gone. And we all said together, "Well I'll be damned."

A family came out of their house to see if they could help. By the light of their flashlight Billy checked the damage and figured out the parts he needed to mount the spare. The four of us pooled our resources, then the farmer took Billy and me to town—which happened to be Noel, of course, seven miles down the road—to get the parts. They cost us almost all we had, and we didn't see one girl. Back at the car Johnny and Jack were waiting for us with the wheel. It had bounced over three fences, they said, and was lying in the middle of a pasture.

By the light of the moon and a kerosene lantern, Billy and the farmer did the fixing while Johnny, Jack, and I drank iced tea and made small talk with the farmer's wife and their two teenage daughters in their kitchen: what we were doing, where we were from, what they raised, what grade everyone was in, what the Elk River was like, what Tulsa was like, etc. The girls were pretty, but nice and shy, not at all like the shameless brazen hussies we had in mind.

Billy and the farmer came in. The wheel was on. We thanked the family for their help and hospitality and walked out to the car. "Oh man, let's go!" Johnny said. "I just hope we're not too late for some action."

"We can't go on," Billy said. "We don't have any

brakes."

"Can't go on? Whatta you mean? We've come this far—it'd be criminal to stop short!"

"We don't have any money, either," I said. "Spent damn near all of it on the parts."

"So what!" Johnny roared. "I'm horny, goddamnit! I want some nooky!"

"We're all horny, buttbrain!" Billy shouted. "But we've got no money, and night's the safest time to drive without brakes, and if you'd rather stay, then goddamnit stay, but it's my fuckin' car and I am goin' back!"

Billy got in the car, Jack and I prepared to push, but Johnny didn't move. I said, "Forget it, John. We were just there and we didn't see one girl. All that nooky we heard about is make-believe." We push-started the car, Johnny and I hopped into the trunk, Jack got in next to Billy. With the emergency brake Billy managed a three-point U turn and headed back toward Tulsa.

Johnny and I were sound asleep when suddenly a god-awful screeching roar startled us off our backs to see millions of sparks flaring into the darkness as the car slowed down and the sparks abated until we finally came to a stop on the shoulder. Silence. Then Johnny said, "I can't fuckin' believe it."

We all got out of the car and walked around it, then Jack said, "I tell ya, if it's not one wheel it's another." We looked and saw what he meant: this time it was the left front that had taken its departure.

Billy announced he'd hitch a ride to Tulsa, which was about fifteen miles away, to get the parts he needed and come right back, and we were to stay and see that no one stole or looted the car. "I don't think you have any reason to worry," Jack said, but we stayed and Billy quickly got a ride. After an hour we crawled through a barbed wire fence and slept in the adjacent field, abandoning the car to looters and thieves. The rising sun woke us up long before we'd gotten enough sleep. The car was still there, unlooted, but no sign of Billy. We breakfasted on peanut butter and jelly sand-wiches, then looked for the wheel for at least an hour, but to no avail, which struck us as downright weird: Jack and Johnny managed to find the first wheel in moonlight, yet the three of us couldn't find the second in broad daylight.

The sun and temperature kept rising. Soon it was hot. There were no trees nearby, so for shade we lay down on the shoulder with our heads and torsos under the car. More and more cars and semis whizzed by us, followed by a hot blast of exhaust-laden after-draft. We wondered what was taking Billy so long. Around noon Johnny announced, "Fuck it. I'm goin' home."

"What about Billy?" I asked. "What about his car and all his stuff?"

"What about him?" Johnny said. "If the car means so much to him, he'd have gotten back hours ago."

"And what about us, Jeff?" Jack said. "The bastard has left us out here high and dry."

"So we leave his dumb-ass car high and dry," Johnny said. "Let's go."

Seemed reasonable to me. We hitched a ride to a gas station in town. I called Mom; she came and got us and took Jack and Johnny home as we told her the story of our trip. "So not only couldn't yall get to Noel, you couldn't even get back to Tulsa," she laughed.

A few days later we learned that when he got home, Billy went to bed. So we had abandoned his car, but he had abandoned us—we were even. We called each other a number of names and laughed the whole thing off.

## A Brief Night at the Drive-In

One evening Jack called Johnny, Rolly, Billy, and me to say his folks had just bought a bitchin' fifty-three Ford station wagon and had given him permission to take it out. He picked us up to go see a movie at the Apache Drive-In.

We all agreed the car was as cool as he had said: turquoise (a very popular color then) with fake wood paneling, a V-eight, and an interior that smelled brand new.

We never paid to go to a drive-in any more than to a regular theater. Instead, we always drove slowly through the exit gate with our lights out hoping no cop was stationed there. More often than not, we got through. If we got caught, the cop merely told us to back out and beat it. Accordingly, on this night Jack started to slowly cruise through the exit gate of the Apache, but then he hit the brakes saying, "There's a chain!"

Immediately the rest of us said, "No there's not! You're seein' things! You're hallucinatin'! Keep goin'! Don't stop! There's nothin' there! You're outa your fuckin' mind!"

"Okay, okay," Jack said, and he put his foot back on the accelerator and we heard a loud crunch and some hair-raising scrape of metal on metal and Jack hit the brakes again, hollering, "You assholes! You said there wasn't a chain!"

As he was backing up, turning around, and gunning it out of there, we were saying, "Damn, Jack, do you believe everthing you hear? You gotta trust your instincts! Think for yourself. Make your own decisions. Forget public opinion. Be your own man."

"Aw shut the fuck up!" Jack said, but, angry and scared as he was, he was also laughing.

He pulled into the first gas station we came to, to survey the damage. He groaned when he saw it. The left front fender was deeply creased, the headlight smashed. "Looks bad, Jack," we all agreed. "Sure glad I'm not in your shoes. Hope you're not grounded for long. Jesus, Jack, didn't your folks just get this car today? Hey, it's not too bad—a headlight and fender is all."

On the verge of tears but laughing, Jack said, "You guys are shit, you know that? Pure-dee shit."

No one disagreed.

### Clap Clap Clap

The fall of my junior year I got a job delivering prescriptions at Getman's Drug Store on East Eleventh (where else?), across the street from the Hudson station where Johnny worked. The other driver was Sid, a tall lean blonde guy who had just finished a tour in the Navy and had the tattoos on his forearms to prove it: a mermaid on one, an anchor entwined by a snake on the other. Sid liked to tell me about the American Legion parties he went to and the stag films he saw there, and after a month he told me about his date the night before with one of the pharmacists, Norma, a reserved woman in her late twenties—told me how he took—well, actually, how he accepted—her virginity, which she eagerly gave up because, he said, under those thick Ivy-League glasses and those subdued Ivy-League sweaters and skirts was a wild woman. I didn't know whether to believe him or not— she exhibited no tell-tale signs, no side glances, no humming or sighing—but I suddenly found I could easily picture a wild and wanton Norma, and me servicing her in Sid's place.

A few weeks later these fantasies petered out because my peter began to hurt, especially when taking a leak—a thick burning sensation that quickly got worse and worse. I felt the pressure to pee more and more often, and when I went it burned increasingly hotter and meaner, until it felt like fishhooks of fire being slowly pulled through my urethra. Finally I described my symptoms to one of the other pharmacists, Bob, a bright, plump, balding guy in his mid-thirties who I got along with. "Jesus, bud," he said, "you've got clap."

"Clap?"

"Gonorrhea."

"Gonorrhea! You mean, like, venereal disease?"

"You got it."

"Holy shit!"

"Who've you been screwin'?"

"Oh, I go to the Carolina now and then."

"That's it. Whores get it all the time. Are you

screwin' anyone else? A girl at school?"

"No."

"Good. Don't, or you'll spread it around yourself. Now go see a doctor. Penicillin will knock it right out. And lay off the whores."

I didn't know any doctors to go to except Dr. Reed. He had taken care of me from my delivery on, had taken my tonsils out and tended my measles and fits of flu and hay fever, and for that reason I didn't want him to know I'd been screwing whores. I mean, he was almost like family, so I asked Bob, "Can't you give me the penicillin?"

"I can't give prescriptions, son. I'm a pharmacist, not a doctor."

"How about playing doctor? I mean, you've got the stuff."

"Break the law on your account? Cause you've been shovin' your tool into prostitutes. C'mon, pal, get serious. Go see a doctor."

I had never made a doctor's appointment myself, and for some reason I didn't want to now. Maybe subconsciously I wanted to confess my sin, to get maternal forgiveness and absolution or something. Whatever my motive, at home that night I told Mom I needed an appointment with Dr. Reed. She asked why. "Oh, for some problems," I said.

"What kind of problems?"

"Oh, personal problems, I guess you could say."

"I see. You've got gonorrhea, haven't you?"

Surprised by her acuity, I saw no reason to lie. "Yes ma'am. But how—"

"When you go to cat houses, Jeffrey, you're going to get clap."

"But how'd you know I've been goin' to—"

"Parents know more than their kids think they do. I just hope you've learned enough to stay away from whores from now on."

"Yes ma'am, I have," I said. "The pain's not worth it."

"Good. I'll call Dr. Reed first thing tomorrow. And you have to pay for the treatment."

She called, I went, and Dr. Reed gave me a shot of penicillin. Seven bucks. He asked who I got it from, so he could report her to the Health Department. I didn't want to snitch, but he pointed out that if I didn't she would only get worse and would give it to others. So, feeling guilty but seeing his point, I told him. He didn't seem surprised. For several days I combed the newspaper to see if the Carolina had been closed down, but, of course, it hadn't. I went back for another shot several days later, and several days later another, and so on until I had spent well over a hundred bucks.

(Years later Mom told me that three or four shots would have been enough, but she told Dr. Reed to make me suffer the pain of paying through the nose in addition to the pain of taking a venereal piss, so I would learn my lesson. And I did. I never touched a whore again.)

Meanwhile, back at work, word got around and the jokes flew right after. "Hey, Jeff, how's your dong doin'? Your hammer hangin'? Your phallus feelin'? Your wee-wee workin'? Your dipstick drippin'?" Etc.

And I'd reply, "It's on the mend. Gonna make a comeback soon, boys and girls. Be in business again bigger and better than ever," I said, hoping.


### The Big Ten Ballroom

On the black radio stations I listened to—for the rhythm and blues, which I much preferred to the diluted white versions of R & B that made the pop charts—I heard about the Big Ten Ballroom on North Apache, in colored town. I hoped someday to go there. In November the station announced a Saturday night extravaganza, with a line-up of twelve acts that included the Clovers, the Five Keys, Bill Dogget, Big Joe Turner, and the like—music I had been listening to for two years. I told Johnny about it, and we decided to go, though with some apprehension. We didn't know how we would be received. But we couldn't miss a show that big.

We told our folks we were going to a party. If we had told them the truth, they would have grounded us in advance: not only were we way underage, but two underage white boys going to a colored joint? We could get arrested, or worse yet get mugged, stabbed, shot. We supposed we could, but we were willing to take a chance that our parents, being grown-ups, weren't.

We dressed up—slacks, sport shirts, sport coats, natty fedoras. We weren't just trying to make a fashion statement; we were also trying to look as old as possible. Had I been going out alone Mom would have kept me in, but in her eyes Johnny could do no wrong, even when he did wrong—like when he occasionally staggered blind-drunk into our house in the middle of the night and fell asleep on the couch because he didn't want to face his father, and Mom thought he was cute even though he was reeking of beer and drooling and snoring like an old man with a cleft palate. So she simply said, "Have a good time, boys—and be careful."

Because I had to work at Getman's till ten, we didn't get to the Big Ten till eleven. It was as advertised, big, but to our surprise, it wasn't a lowdown, warehouse-like joint, as we had expected; it was a really nice Art Deco structure, though we didn't know that term at the time. At the door we paid a ten buck cover charge. The man said that for an extra fifteen we could have a table close to the stage. We handed him a ten and a five and a lovely young woman led us into the ballroom. It was packed—I'd say a good two thousand people were there, if not more—and with a few exceptions like John and me, they were black. And oh how they were dressed, not loud and flashy according to stereotype, but subtly, in fabrics soft and subdued, the men in suits and sport coats, the women in form-fitting dresses that were flattering without being vulgar. On the stage a big band was jamming. We asked which act this was. "Oh, this is the warm-up band," our hostess said; "the main show hasn't started yet." Johnny and I looked at each other and grinned: this was our kind of place.

She led us to a vacant table in the second row. After she explained how the Big Ten did business, we ordered a setup—i.e., a bucket of ice and Seven-Up—and a bootlegger. In a matter of minutes a short fat black guy in a double-breasted beige suit was at our table. Because we were running out of money fast, we bought the smallest of the cheapest he had—a half-pint of Jim Beam for eleven bucks. (Which brought our total up to about forty bucks, in 1955!) Johnny and I mixed ourselves a drink and noticed a slim black guy in his early twenties sitting between our table and the next who seemed to be alone. We asked him if he'd like a drink—why, he'd be much obliged—so we introduced ourselves to each other—James the name, fun's my game—and in no time, fun being our game as well, we were pals.

When our bottle was empty James produced his, a full pint, and who the hell needed Seven-Up with Wild Turkey? Soon we were sharing James's bottle with folks at adjacent tables, and they were sharing theirs with us. Even in the latrine a bottle would be passed down the line as we were all taking our whizzes and saying things like, "Praise the Lord and pass the ammunition. Keep it movin', keep it movin'. Thank you, brother. Mmmmm, mmmm, mmmm, now that is fine shit!" The whole night was like that: share and share alike, with no holding out on those who had less (like Johnny and me), and no holding back by those who had more.

The only discordant note in all this music and whisky harmony came early on: an older black woman sitting behind us muttering, "What're them white boys doin' here anyway? Why don't they stay where they belong? Who the hell asked them here, anyway?" Finally James turned and said, "Hush now, Mama—these boys aren't botherin' you, so leave 'em alone, y'hear?" Others around seconded James's motion, and the old woman complained no more.

And as we shared the whiskey, so we shared the music. The main acts began around midnight, and we all danced and sang along, and between acts shared whiskey and cigarettes and observations and jokes and lies, then danced and sang along with the next act, utterly abandoning ourselves to the music in a euphoria of rhythmic motion and panting breathlessness and sweat, becoming the music, becoming the dance, becoming in a way pure body, out of our minds—until finally, by show's end at six in the morning, we were sweat-drenched and exhausted, and everyone laughed and hugged and wished each other well.

On the way home, Johnny said, "Wasn't that the greatest, Jay? Was that not absolutely the greatest?" And this time around, unlike the night of his party and the night we lost our cherries, I was able in all honesty to agree.

### *The Grocery Business*

While I was working at Getman's another buddy of mine, Jim Gower, sold me a car off of his dad's used-car lot. Jim was cursed with a face that looked like a blend of James Dean and Paul Newman, and the girls fell all over themselves falling all over him. Cursed, you ask? For a guy as shy as Jim, even so. Without a few drinks he didn't feel comfortable even with his pals, and he never felt comfortable with girls, especially when they were going ga-ga over his face.

Jim was never a sosh or a jock. He was not a sterling student, nor was he a hood. In junior and senior high he was always on the outskirts of the student body, doing his own thing: prepping and selling cars for his dad; playing golf, not on the school team, but with grownups he somehow met who liked to gamble; going out and getting drunk and occasionally getting into fights (he was small but tough as scrap-iron). He didn't participate in one school activity that I know of. He was always his own man, Jim, keeping to himself even when he was with his friends. Which is why, though we had known each other since seventh grade, Jim and I didn't hang around with each other until I was no longer doing sports. Because from then on, when I was not a jock or a sosh, much less a student leader or a hood—when, like Jim, I didn't fit into any clique—why then, I was on the outskirts as well. So Jim and I, often with Rolly and John, spent our money and leisure at various bars and juke joints, both white and black.

Jim sold me a two-door olive-green forty-nine Ford for three hundred and twenty-five dollars. Mom didn't want me to buy it, but since I was working, it seemed to me, especially after Jim sweet-talked me, that I needed something to show for my time and labor. Instead of a letter on a jacket, a car on the street. I didn't have the money, but with Mom's co-signature I got a loan. My payments were twenty-five dollars a month. They were the reason Mom finally co-signed: she figured the discipline of payments would do me good. Three months after I got the car Sid got in a wreck, Getman's insurers said they would no longer cover drivers under twenty-five, so I was out of a job. I had to get another right away or else lose the car, which brings me to the grocery business.

Supermarkets employed a lot of teenagers, so I inquired at one after another. To my dismay, some paid as little as sixty cents an hour, and none needed my help. Finally the manager of Sipe's—a local upscale chain—hesitated before saying no. His hesitation was my cue. As per Mom's wisdom, I went back several days in a row until I finally broke him down. The pay was the same as Getman's, seventy-five cents an hour, but I got to work only two hours after school and ten on Saturday, which meant a pay cut of fifty percent. But sixteen bucks a week was better than nothing.

I was a bagger. Bagging was fairly heavy work—nothing like construction, of course, but compared to driving a fifty-five V-eight Ford and carrying little sacks of pills to front doors, it amounted to hard labor. Because not only did we put the groceries in paper bags, we carried the bags out to the customer's car. In addition to this service I also provided the customers pleasant and what I hoped was witty conversation in hopes of getting tips. And sometimes I did.

When business was slow I helped stock the shelves. Stocking was easier than bagging, but, I quickly discovered, it involved an occupational hazard. When I reached into a box for a bottle of olives or jelly or ketchup or whatever, I often hit the divider, which cut my cuticles and produced a set of hangnails that hurt something fierce. Bandaids helped, but I would inadvertently tear them off, and since I couldn't spend all my time taping my fingers, I would carry on and slice my cuticles some more, cuts on top of cuts, cuts within cuts.

Soon I ran into a problem, this other kid who worked at Sipe's, an irritatingly cheerful, goody-two-shoes kind of guy named Herb who often, I shit you not, actually whistled while he worked. The manager loved Herb, even though he gold-bricked big-time. He moved around a lot, but actually accomplished little. It bugged me. Couldn't the manager see what Herb was doing?

I decided to deal with this problem—which was a problem only because I made it one, of course—by showing Herb up. From the stockroom I started taking out loads that were obviously half again as large as his, which I unloaded twice as fast as he unloaded his, then I'd take a conspicuous break in the stockroom, enjoying a coke and a smoke, and sometimes a sandwich as well. One evening the manager came into the stockroom where I was busy showing Herb up.

"What're you doing?" he asked.

"Eatin' a sandwich."

"Why aren't you stocking?" he asked.

"I finished my load."

"You don't see Herb taking an unauthorized break," he said.

"He hasn't finished his dinky little load, either."

"Oh. I see," he said, but I could tell by his tone that he didn't see, not my way at least.

Then another issue arose. The manager decided that everyone, even baggers, should wear a white shirt and a tie. I deemed the idea inane, and to make my point I began grooming and dressing like a hood, clumping around in the kind of black boots that Harley bikers favored, combing my hair into ducktails, and wearing dark-colored shirts with the collar turned halfway up my neck and the front unbuttoned halfway down my hairy chest (to wow the women, who, alas, never seemed to even notice, much less proposition me). The manager reminded me a few times of his policy; I reminded him that I was doing my job damn well thank you. After two or three weeks of flagrant dress-code disobedience and indirect demonstrations of Herb's gold-bricking, I had made my points so well that I got, to use a term of the trade, sacked.

## A Quick Trip to Oklahoma City

At the beginning of our junior year, Jack's family moved to Oklahoma City. It took a while before we could visit him: Rolly was playing football, Billy was wrestling, Johnny and I were working weekends—only Jim was free. Come January, though, all of us except Billy found a free weekend. Deciding we'd never find a time when everyone was free, and considering that Billy didn't drink anyway, the four of us decided to pay Jack a call, especially since he was wrestling that Friday night.

We took my car. To see Jack in action we had to hustle, but we could just make it thanks to the recently constructed Turner Turnpike, which ran non-stop between Tulsa and Oklahoma City. I floored it all the way, ninety-five miles an hour. About half way there we ran into rain. I turned on the windshield wipers. They worked fine for a minute or two, but then they went spastic, randomly twitching and lurching, sometimes even flopping around on the windshield like landed fish, as if they were a Laurel-and-Hardy gag, but the comedy posed a serious problem: I could hardly see. Yet I couldn't slow down if we were to see Jack wrestle.

From the back seat Jim instructed Johnny to reach way up under the dash and feel for a couple of slender metal arms, one left of the dashboard's center, one right. Sitting on the very edge of the front seat with his right knee on the floor, his right cheek on the dashboard, and his right arm buried to his shoulder, Johnny groped around until he felt the arms. They were barely attached to a motor that was rotating them, he said. "Yep," Jim said, "that's the problem. So turn 'em off, Jeff, and Johnny, you push the arm for the left wiper back and forth."

"By hand?" hollered Johnny.

"Well, not by foot!" Jim answered. "We haven't got time to stop and fix it."

So, as I barreled down the turnpike in pelting rain, Johnny worked the wiper manually until his arm gave out, then he and Jim traded places and Jim worked the wiper, then Jim and Rolly traded places so Rolly could take a turn, and so it went all the way to Jack's high school. We were just in time to see him lose. Afterwards, as we were driving to Jack's favorite bar, he said, "You know, fellas, I think it might help if I got into shape." We pointed out that getting into shape was for pipsqueaks and sissies, then we all got tanked.

Next morning we enjoyed a big breakfast and a visit with Jack's folks. His mother was pretty and southern-style vivacious—she called Jack "Jackie"—and his father was baby-faced and fat like Jack, but even so, he was a very low handicap golfer who could sprint backwards almost as fast as we could forwards. We were leaving to explore the town— i.e., to check out some other bars—when Johnny's mother called to say that the weather people were predicting more rain that would by afternoon turn into sleet—we should head on back to Tulsa right away. A mist was blowing in at the time, and the thermometer outside the Walcotts' kitchen window was down to thirty-five, so Jim fixed the windshield wipers and, reluctantly, we started back. On the Walcotts' advice we took Highway 66 instead of the turnpike—there would be less traffic, the traffic would be slower and therefore safer, and there would be businesses along the way in case we ran into trouble.

They must have been clairvoyant.

Soon after we were out of town we got a blowout— the right front tire. Johnny said, "Yall stay here—I'll take care of it."

"No, man, we'll—"

He stopped us short, yelling, "Goddamnit, I have a hangover and need to work it off, so shut the fuck up and stay put!" He jumped out of the car, stripped to the waist, and in the cold driving mist, while the rest of us sat in the car and watched, he grabbed the jack, the lug wrench, and the spare out of the trunk, jacked the car up, pried off the hubcap, took off the flat tire, mounted the spare, let down the car, threw the flat tire, the hubcap, and the tools into the trunk, and jumped back into the car, all in maybe three minutes. We had never seen him move so fast.

"Feel better?" we asked.

"Lot better," he said, panting, shivering, his skin goose-bumped and blue.

I pulled into the next gas station to get the flat fixed. This was before tubeless steel-belted tires hit the scene, so when you had a flat you had to get the inner tube patched. Filling stations usually charged a buck for one patch, plus twenty-five cents apiece for additional patches.

With the flat fixed we had a spare and took off again for Tulsa. Maybe fifteen minutes later we had another flat— the right rear. This time, as I was pulling over onto the shoulder, everyone was laughing and saying things like, "This is gittin' old. Do sumpn interesting for a change, Jeff. Throw a rod. Hit a deer." Johnny did his racing-car pit-stop routine, we got the flat fixed at the next gas station, and again headed for Tulsa. By now the mist was turning into a fine sleet. It wasn't icing the surface yet, but it soon would be.

A few minutes later we had another flat—the left rear —and another chorus: "Jesus, Jeff, you buy your tubes at the Salvation Army? Fuckin' cheapskate. Fuckin' menace, you mean. Endangerin' life and limb. There oughta be a law." Johnny did his thing, we got the flat fixed, headed northeast again, and about thirty minutes later the left front tire went kaput and yet another chorus commenced. "What's next? The transmission gonna fall out? Naw, the motor. Can a radiator have a flat? Duncan's can. I think I'm gonna walk— I ain't got all year."

Johnny changed the wheel and we pulled into the next filling station to get the flat fixed. Only this time, as my buddies went to the bar next door for a beer, I went with the fairly young, chunky, dull-eyed pump jockey into the garage. My heart sank when I saw the inner tube he pulled out of the tire—it had so many red patches it looked like it had acne. He inflated it, sank it into a tank of water and a string of bubbles issued forth. He patched the hole and was about to stuff the tube back into the tire when I said, "You wanta check to see if there's another?"

"Oh yeah," he said, and quickly found another. After he fixed that one he was going to stuff the tube into the tire when I stopped him again. "Oh yeah," he said, and found and fixed yet another. This time, though, all on his own he checked and found several leaks. The two of us stared at the tube in his hands, then I got an idea. "Yall carry used tubes?" He checked and found one the right size with only one patch. He inflated and tested it—no leaks. "Whatta you charge for used tubes?" A quarter, he said. "Sold," I replied. He installed the tube and laid the wheel in the trunk. I gave him a quarter, said thanks, fetched the boys from the bar, and, slowly, very carefully, the road being slippery with sleet now, I drove to Tulsa without any more flats. And we all laughed that I had pulled such a fast one, getting a tube for a quarter after the guy had done almost two dollars worth of work.

140          *Low Crimes and Misdemeanors*

I shouldn't have felt good about taking advantage of a guy who was a little slow, I know that—but I did.

### A Double Date

After getting fired from Sipe's I got a job at Rayco Seat Covers, located on (you guessed it) East Eleventh. One of the guys who worked there was Harold Story. Harold was deaf, but he was rock-and-roll cool. Short and wiry, with black hair that he combed into ducktails, he wore long sideburns, a pack of Luckies in the left sleeve-roll of his white T-shirt, Levi's with a sharp crease front and back, white socks, and black wingtip shoes with taps on the heels and toes. Harold drove a car of equal style, an always-immaculate white, fifty-two Ford convertible with white walls, fender skirts, dual pipes with glass-pack mufflers, red vinyl tuck-and-roll upholstery, and a pair of angora dice hanging from the rearview mirror. Harold had a very cute girl friend name of Judy who was also deaf. Judy could read lips and talk. Harold could talk only enough to call me Jeppey, which became my Rayco nickname; other than that he used sign language, of which I learned enough to engage in a little Tarzan-Tonto conversation: Me Jeppey. You Harold. We friends. You like beer? Me like beer too.

Occasionally Harold, Judy, and I went out together, to drink and dance. (Deaf folks feel the percussion.) One time we double-dated to the Admiral Drive-In. It was my first date with a good-looking girl I met somehow, somewhere, some-time or other—I don't remember, any more than I remember her name. I didn't tell her that the couple we were going with was deaf. She was taken aback by our chatter in broken English and pidgin sign. Now, Harold and Judy went to the Admiral all the time, but, having no need of a speaker, they parked outside the cyclone fence in the back. However, I wanted a speaker, and I was sure my date did too. But I didn't want to pay, of course, so, to my date's horror—I don't think that's too strong a word—I told Harold and Judy how to sneak in through the exit. Judy and he clapped their hands and laughed, not just in approval, but in glee. My date, on the other hand, despite my reassurances, softly moaned and whimpered at the prospect of being arrested, handcuffed, thrown in jail, and dealing with her irate parents.

Harold idled through the exit, lights off. When we were about fifteen yards past the gate, a fat cop stepped in front of us. Harold stopped. My date shrank into the back corner of the passenger's side, not moaning or whimpering now, just petrified. The cop walked to Harold's window, shone his flashlight on Harold's face, and said, "Okay, buddy, just turn around and go straight back out, y'hear?"

Harold pointed to his ear, shook his head, and said, "Aaaa-ooooaaaa."

"Aw shit," the cop muttered, then turned his light on Judy. "Look, sis, yall gotta go back where you came from, you understand?"

Judy pointed to her ear, shook her head, and said, "Ooooo-aaaaaoooo."

"Oh for God's sake," the cop growled, then turned his light on me. "Alright, Red, you tell him to—"

Before he finished I pointed to my ear, shook my head, and said, "Eeeeee-aaaaooo."

The cop stared at us a moment, then said, "Aw fuck it" and waved us on in. Harold and Judy laughed and congratulated me on my acting and my presence of mind. My date, on the other hand, sulked the rest of the night, staying as far away from me as she could get. She didn't even watch the movie.

Another relationship nipped in the bud.


### *A Sunday Afternoon at Ft. Gibson Lake*

It was a beautiful spring day, warm, full of blue sky, soft air, and flowers—jonquils, red buds, dogwoods. A

142                            *Low Crimes and Misdemeanors*

perfect day, Johnny and I agreed, to go to the lake. Maybe fish. With some luck maybe we'd run into someone we knew with a boat and do some skiing. With a lot of luck run into a couple of girls and get laid. (Like a dog at a dinner table, we never gave up hope.)

I drove. We parked at a dock-cum-boat launch and watched a number of folks—no one we knew—back their outboards down the concrete ramp into the water. Anchored here and there were Lone Star aluminum row boats that you could put a small outboard on. Empty, they were bobbing like corks in little ripples and wavelets that slapped the sides and made a kind of metallic music. A guy we liked a lot but never hung around with drove up—Denny Lyle. He parked his creampuff, robin's-egg-blue, thirty-eight, four-door Oldsmobile and joined us. He too had decided the day was too nice to spend in town. We sat on the front fenders and bumper of his car soaking up the light, the warmth, the color, the fragrance—honeysuckle mixed with engine exhaust—and talking about mutual acquaintances and Denny's heart. Denny had a heart condition that kept him out of sports—the reason we never became buddies—and when we saw him we always asked him about it, in hopes it hadn't gotten worse. It hadn't.

Then Johnny walked down to the dock and jumped into one of the empty rowboats. Carefully stepping from one cross-member to the next, he walked the length of the boat from stern to bow, then leaped into another. Both boats slipped and slid a little, but Johnny managed to keep his balance. By this time everyone was watching him, to his straight-faced delight. He walked the length of that boat and jumped into another. This time a number of people applauded. He repeated the stunt again, a longer jump, and everyone cheered. By now he was near a houseboat. The people on it said, "Jump on board, kid, and we'll give you a beer."

"You're on!" he shouted, then leaped, only this time the boat slipped out from under him and he belly-flopped into the water. Everyone laughed.

He hauled himself out of the water, took a few bows and curtsies, then walked over to Denny and me. To dry Johnny and his clothes, Denny suggested driving around while Johnny sat on the fender. After we had been slowly cruising back-country roads for fifteen, twenty minutes, Denny and I in the car chatting, Johnny on the right front fender airing, Denny slammed on the brakes to avoid a squirrel and sent Johnny flying into the air and landing on the road, rolling and laughing in the dirt and gravel.

Well, hell's bells, Johnny couldn't have all the fun, so I jumped out of the car and up on the right fender while Johnny got back up on the left, and Denny, understanding the game without a word, took off. The rule was the same as the one on the golf carts at Highland years before: Johnny and I couldn't hold on to anything while Denny did everything he could—suddenly stopping, swerving this way and that, abruptly starting stopping starting stopping—to throw us sprawling and rolling in dirt and gravel and weeds. He also brushed against bushes and tree limbs to knock us off or make us jump.

After a couple hours or so, Denny dropped us off back at the dock. He said the fun was worth the scrapes and scratches his car got, and Johnny and I agreed it was worth the scrapes and scratches our bodies got. We were both dirty as could be, but with a difference: I was dust-dirty, while Johnny was mud-dirty. I took my shirt and pants off and beat them against a tree, while Johnny jumped into the lake with his clothes on and thrashed around to simulate a washing machine. I put my shirt and pants back on while John took his off for the journey home. He rolled the back windows up to hold his laundry so it would dry in the wind. Once on the highway he also took off his underwear and held it out the window. I asked, "Where the hell are your hairs, man?"

"Had to shave 'em off. I got crabs"

"Where in hell'd you git crabs?"

"Probly the Carolina."

"So why'd you shave your hairs?"

"That's what you do—shave 'em off and smear Amelia's Blue Ointment on. But let me tell you, Jay, layin' down at night, I can't find any position where my pecker's not gittin' scraped by crotch whiskers, and that's as bad as the itchin' from the damn crabs." Then he looked down at his crotch. "So feast away while you can, you little sonsabitches, cause your days are numbered!"

We joked about the fruits of our venereal labors at the Carolina all the way back home. In a few weeks Johnny finally got rid of his crabs, and he never went back. Like me and the clap, once was enough.

### Malicious Tampering

After school one fine spring afternoon (there's no season like spring for getting into trouble) Billy and I drove over from Will Rogers to our barbershop, the Casa Loma, which was in the same little strip of shops as T.G.&Y and Crawford Drug Store, across Eleventh from the Royal Theater and across Columbia Street from our old junior high, Woodrow Wilson. Everyone went to the Casa Loma because you didn't just get a haircut there—you hung out and gossiped and lagged quarters on the sidewalk in front and listened to ball games on the radio or watched them on TV and talked sports and made bets with the bootblack, Hoss, who in a little black notebook made book on every sporting event in America, it seemed. In the narrow parking lot behind the string of stores I parked my car next to a little Harley. It had a one-twenty-five cc engine, as I recall, and a hand clutch and foot shift, to compete with the little bikes from overseas.

Billy noticed that the ignition had not been locked, so he turned the switch, kick-started the engine, and drove it from one end of the parking lot to the other several times, then pulled up to me and said, "You've gotta try it, man—

it's downright cute." I was driving it back and forth from one end of the lot to the other when out of the back door of a beauty shop burst a trim little man wearing a short white jacket and curly black hair screaming, "I caught you, you goddamned thieves!" I stopped as a cop car pulled into the lot at one end and a second pulled in at the other. "Here they are, officers!" the man screamed, grabbing the handlebars. "Arrest them! I caught 'em red handed stealing my motorcycle!"

"We're not stealin' your damn motorcycle," I said.

"You saw him, officer," the man said. "And this one"—indicating Billy—"took it first!"

"I *drove* it," Billy said. "I didn't fuckin' *take* it, goddamnit—I *drove* it!"

One of the cops spoke up. "But you've got no right to drive it, son. It's not yours."

"Yeah?" Billy said. "And he shouldn't leave the damn ignition unlocked."

"You're right," the other cop said, "but that still doesn't give yall the right to take a joy ride on someone else's bike. Git in the car."

"What for?" I asked. "It's obvious we weren't tryin' to steal it."

"Malicious tampering," the first cop said.

"What the hell is that?" Billy demanded.

"Messin' around with someone else's property," number two cop said.

"We weren't messing around with it maliciously," I argued.

"Just shut up and git in the car, Red," number two said, gesturing to his car.

We got in the back seat of his car and he drove us to the station downtown where some other cops fingerprinted us, took our wallets and belts and keys, then led us up a flight of stairs and locked us in what they explained was a juvenile detention cell right next to the women's quarters, which were behind a big, windowless, metal door. Our cell was right out of the movies: bars in front facing a blank cinder-block wall across a narrow corridor, a bench bed suspended by chains hooked into the wall, a toilet in the back. It was dark like a cave and stank of piss and disinfectant. We asked if we could call home—they said they would take care of all that. We could hear some women hollering and sometimes laughing, but we had no idea what they were saying or laughing about.

After a couple of hours we were taken downstairs to an office where Billy's mother was waiting. Ordinarily Mrs. Crowder and I got along, but at that moment she glared at me and yelled, "I don't want you around Billy ever again, Jeffrey Duncan! You're always getting him into trouble!" I almost laughed. *I* got *Billy* into trouble? How about *him* getting *me* into trouble? In truth, we could, and often did, manage to get into trouble quite well on our own but, feeling that talk would be useless, I said nothing.

She had come to take Billy home. The cops thought she had come to take me as well, but she corrected their mistake rather emphatically, so, while Billy went home with his mother, I spent the night in the cell by myself wondering why my mother hadn't come to get me. It was godawful lonely and boring, being in jail. There was nothing to do—no radio, no TV, no books or magazines, no paper, pen, or pencil. And the only people I saw for the next eighteen hours or so were the ones who brought me dinner and breakfast, and they refused to answer any of my questions. All there was to do was think, and like most seventeen year olds (I guess), I had nothing much to think about. Except sex, but after jacking off I found sex about as interesting to contemplate as a budget.

Around noon the next day a cop took me downstairs to an office where Mom was waiting. She was stone-faced, silent. When a cop brought me my wallet and belt and keys, she thanked him and walked out of the office. I followed her out of the station, to the parking lot, into the car. She drove me home in silence.

In the house she said, "I want you to know that I had to post a fifteen hundred dollar bond to get you out of jail. I had to borrow it from Brant Miller. I want you to think about that, asking him for fifteen hundred dollars to spring my son from jail, the same son I had to ask him to drive a hundred miles to bring home from McAlester last year. You owe him a lot."

"I'll pay it back," I said.

"I don't mean the money. We'll get it back—it's bond money, not a fine. What I mean is the interest he's taken in you, the time and trouble, and there doesn't seem to be any improvement. Same for me: I want to be proud of you, Jeffrey, but how can I when you pull a stunt like this?"

"I don't know," I said.

"I don't either," she said. "But I hope you've learned something from this. I could have gotten you out last night, but I wanted you to spend some time there, to see what it's like."

"It stinks," I said.

"Good!"

"But I gotta say," I said, "that gittin' tossed in jail just for ridin' around on that guy's bike seems outa proportion. It was obvious we weren't tryin' to steal it."

"I didn't say what you did was bad, Jeffrey. It was just stupid. Stupid enough to deserve a night in jail."

"So what're you gonna do to me?"

"For punishment? I'm going to hope that a night in jail is punishment enough."

"What're *they* gonna do to me?"

"I don't know. But I'll tell you this: whatever they decide will be fine by me."

As it turned out, the police must have concluded the whole affair was, as Billy and I had suggested, a whole lot of form with very little content, because they did nothing to either of us: no day in court, no reprimand, no warning, nothing. And Mom must have agreed with them, because she didn't say another word about the episode. But if Billy and I

148          *Low Crimes and Misdemeanors*

had actually stolen the motorcycle, I guarantee you she would have told them to send me to reform school.

### *Thievery*

Not that I didn't steal on occasion. Once I had a paper route I was responsible for buying my own clothes. Preferring to spend my money on alcohol and tobacco and juke joints, I stole my shirts, underwear, and socks by slipping them under my shirt or jacket. I didn't try stealing pants, shoes, or coats—they were too bulky, too risky.

And I actually did steal a motorcycle, with Billy—it was an Indian, a make that was no longer in production. It sat in front of a house on our street for two or three weeks in the exact same place, which meant to us that since it was not being driven and it was parked in a public place, it was, by our definition if not the law's, public property. It had some parts Billy could use, so late one night we pushed it down the alley and parked it behind my garage—a place where no one ever looked—and Billy stripped it of the parts he wanted. It sat there for a few days until we figured we were pushing our luck, so late one night Billy towed it out of town with his thirty-eight Chevy coupe as I steered it and we dumped it in the still waters of a gravel pit.

In the Delman Theater parking lot one Sunday afternoon, Billy and I grabbed a lug wrench out of my car and in broad daylight swiped a couple of spare wheels mounted on the sides of a pickup truck because they were perfect for the hotrod he was turning his Chevy into. We threw them in the trunk of my car, drove around the block, parked in the same lot, and snuck in to see the movie.

On occasion Jim, Rolly, Billy, Johnny, and I— usually in some combination of two or three, rarely all of us at once, on account of space—would drive at night into the alley behind the Dr. Pepper bottling plant on Eleventh and load the car with cases of empties that were stacked alongside the building. Then we'd drive to gas stations and grocery stores to sell them. I especially remember the expression on the shopkeeper's face one night when he saw, as Jim and I carried in case after case of empties, that he had without realizing it agreed to buy thirty-five of them. At two cents a bottle that's sixteen dollars and eighty cents, a pretty substantial sum when gas cost twenty-five cents a gallon.

North Pine was lined with salvage yards. One kept a huge mound of batteries just inside the gate of the driveway and just out of sight of the office window. Once in a while Billy and I would drive there, park in the lot, walk through the gate, pick up a battery each, and carry them to the office where we got paid two bucks apiece. The money was nice, but even nicer was the idea, which we found unfailingly hilarious, that they were paying us for their own batteries.

A few times several of us happened to be in the parking lot behind a bar as a beer truck pulled in to make a delivery. Need I say what we did when the driver pushed his hand truck loaded with cases of beer into the bar? No, I don't, but I should say that we looked at the situation like this: to turn down such an opportunity would be like thumbing our noses at Providence, and we didn't want to do that.

### *A Crazy Ride on Highway 66*

One Sunday night Johnny and I went to the Hi Way 66 Drive-In in the beat-up forty-one Chevy that his folks let him take turns driving with his brother Jack. (Their dad would not let them have a car of their own even if they paid for it, insisting that the Chevy did them just fine.) That night was Johnny's turn.

He drove quickly through the exit, and after he had

parked and had mounted the speaker in the window, he reached up and grabbed a corner of the torn headliner, ripped off a big piece, and wiped the windshield inside and out. Inasmuch as the headliner was fifteen years old, Johnny's efforts only spread the dirt on the windshield into a thick smear. We watched the movie as if through a mud-slide, which we decided made it far more interesting by increasing the suspense—we had to wonder not only what would happen, but also what the hell was happening at that very moment. When it ended Johnny drove off with the speaker still in the window, ripping the cord out of the post and explaining that he had always wanted a crappy drive-in speaker.

We drove into Tulsa on Eleventh which happened to be empty of any cars except the Chevy. We had never seen Eleventh empty before, and Johnny had this bright idea. He straddled the center line and started turning the steering wheel so that we were swerving back-and-forth. In a moment of inspiration, Johnny lifted his hands and what do you know?—the wheel kept turning back and forth all by itself. Further, the arcs it described got larger and larger, until we were swerving from one side of the street clear over to the other—four lanes, curb-to-curb.

Grabbing the wheel, Johnny stopped the car in the middle of the street. Then he took off, pulled the wheel hard to the left, and let go. The car did it again. Johnny climbed up into the window, his head and torso outside the car, while I, now sitting in the middle of the bench seat, managed the accelerator with my left foot. As for steering wheel and brakes, who needed 'em? The street was all ours. And so we slalomed down Highway 66 until once again we were going curb-to-curb. Johnny dropped back into the car, stopped in the middle of the street, and we traded places. I took off, then got up in the window while he managed the accelerator as the car did its nutty thing, which was as hilarious as driving the golf carts at Highland and riding Denny Lyle's car at Ft. Gibson Lake.

Then we heard the siren, saw the flashing red light. I dropped from the window into the driver's seat and pulled over into a closed gas station. The cop car pulled in right behind me. We got out and instantly two short, hard-breathing cops were throwing us against the Chevy, roughing us up and yelling, "You crazy sonsabitches! You tryin to git someone killed!"

Johnny and I protested, "But the street was empty!"

"Jesus H. Christ!" the bald one cried. "Someone coulda pulled in from a side street! A car or a bike! A pedestrian!"

"At midnight on Sunday?" I exclaimed.

"Well *you're* out, aintcha?" the potbellied one said, "so why not someone else? Let's see your licenses."

Johnny and I showed him our licenses, then Baldy said, "Well well well, what have we here?" He was standing behind the car, peering into the trunk he had opened, playing his flashlight around on a pile of assorted hub caps, mixed in with several lug wrenches and tire irons. "What you boys got to say about this?" Baldy asked.

"I didn't know those were there," Johnny said.

"You expect us to believe that'?" Potbelly said.

"If I was stealin' hub caps," Johnny said. "I wouldn't keep the evidence in the car."

"If I stole hub caps," I added, "I'd steal sets, not one here and one there."

"Well well well, lookey what I found under the driver's seat." Baldy again. He was standing by the driver's door, holding up two whiskey bottles, pints that were partially filled. Johnny and I looked at each other, shocked. "What you boys got to say about these?"

"I didn't know those were there, either," Johnny said.

"For the love o' God," Potbelly said, "who're you tryin' to kid?"

"If we'd known they were there," I said, "we'd've been drinkin' 'em! You can believe that, can't you?"

"Just smell our breath," Johnny added. "We haven't

152 *Low Crimes and Misdemeanors*

had a drop."

They looked at us for a few seconds. I prepared myself for a night in jail and multiple charges—reckless driving, illegal possession of alcohol and stolen goods. Plus parental wrath. High school expulsion. Reform school. Skid Row. Then Baldy said, "You boys git on outa here and behave yourselves, ya hear?"

"Yes sir," we answered.

Potbelly added, as he stashed the bottles in their car, "You better, cause if we see yall screwin' around like that again, you're gonna git it with both barrels."

"Yes sir," we replied. As Johnny drove me home, we wondered why they let us off. The only reason we could come up with was the credibility of our logic and the innocence of our breath. But we also wondered if they hadn't gotten a kick out of seeing a car with a kid sitting in the driver's window careering back and forth like a skier sweeping down Highway 66.

We also wondered what Johnny's brother Jack had been up to when he had the car.

## *A Week Off*

One fine Friday morning in the merry month of May I noticed in my first class, English, that a number of students, the type who were never absent, were absent. I asked a classmate what was going on. She said it was Journalism Day at T.U. Journalism Day? She explained: it was a conference for all the high school students in Tulsa who were taking and/or were going to take journalism. I was miffed. I had signed up for journalism the next year, and I hadn't heard a thing about this Journalism Day. Not that I was all that interested in attending a conference, but I was always interested in cutting school, and besides, Amy—a nice-looking, very witty girl who had the brass to wear big bold glasses and who I was quite interested in, one could say—

this Amy wasn't in class and I figured she might be at the conference. I went to the teacher, a young guy named Ronald McKenzie straight out of Oklahoma State who I got along with, and explained the situation. (Okay, I explained part of the situation; I didn't say anything about Amy.) (Okay, I probably didn't have to say anything about Amy: he was no dummy.) McKenzie agreed that I should go to the conference and gave me a pass to see the Junior Class Counselor.

Miss Calhoun—a forty-ish, serious, thick-waisted, thick-lipped, school-teachery sort of woman aptly named Edwina—pulled a sheet of paper out of a drawer and explained that it was a list of the students who had been given permission to attend the conference, and that my name wasn't on it. I suggested she write my name on it. She explained that the permission had to be granted by two days ago. I pointed out that I didn't know about the conference, otherwise I'd have asked for permission several *weeks* ago. She said that the event had been publicized well in advance, and if I wasn't absent so much I would have heard of it. I noted that my absences were excused. (Explanation: when I wanted to skip school, which I did at least once every other week, I'd go to school a little early and get a girl—which wasn't hard because so many of them liked the thrill of breaking some rules—to call the attendance office from the booth of the pay phone right across the hall and, speaking as Mrs. Duncan, ask the attendant to excuse my absence that day, I was sick.) Miss Calhoun explained that to get permission one had to hand in a card signed by all one's teachers certifying that one was passing all one's classes. As it happened, I was passing all my classes at the time, so I explained that she could give me a card which I could take to my teachers who would sign it and then she could add my name to the list and I could go. She explained that as she'd already explained, the card was due two days ago. I explained that as I had explained, I didn't know about the event otherwise I would have handed a card in. She explained that not knowing was my tough luck, that if, as she had already

154        *Low Crimes and Misdemeanors*

explained, I graced the school with my presence a little more often, I would have known, so her answer was no, permission denied, case closed, get back to class.

Rigid bureaucracy, and by-the-book bureaucrats, drove me nuts. (Still do.) Therefore, from Miss Calhoun's office I walked straight to my car, drove straight to the Student Union at T.U., found Amy, attended a couple of sessions and the luncheon with her, then talked her into skipping the afternoon sessions so we could spend the rest of this gorgeous spring day outside. We went to the zoo where we teased the animals and ate hotdogs and fries. That evening we rejoined our fellow journalists for a free movie downtown at the Orpheum. We had a very nice time. Amy said she didn't know I could be so nice. I said I didn't either. She asked if it was nice being nice for a change. I said with her it was. She said good.

Next Monday I got to school a little early, went straight to Hipsher's office and waited for him in the ante-room. When he arrived he looked at me a second, then asked, "You here to see me?" I said I was. "Well, come in and have a seat." I followed him into his office and had a seat. "So, Jeffrey," he said, sitting down behind his desk, "to what do I owe the surprise, not to speak of the pleasure, of this visit?" I told him what I had done. "I see. And you came here to save me the trouble of sendin' for you, is that it?" I said it was. "Why, you are the very soul of courtesy and consideration." I said I tried to be. He smiled, looked at me for a few seconds, then shook his head. "You know I'm gonna have to suspend you." I said I knew. "But it's not going to be an ordinary suspension." I said I believed I could handle an extraordinary suspension. "Oh I'm sure you can. Now, you've been payin' me a lotta calls the last couple of months, disruptin' damn near every class you're in time and again, and I've been mighty patient, I think you'll agree." I said I agreed. "But patience hasn't done spit in the way of improvin' your behavior. And to be frank, Jeffrey, much as I enjoy your society, too much of a good thing... you know." I said I knew. "So here's the deal: I'm suspending you indefinitely. That means you can come back to school tomorrow, next week, next month, next year, or never. It's up to you." I said really? "Really. Only there's a catch. If and when you come back, by God you better be *ready* to come back, because if I see you in this office again, I'll expel you. You want to go to college, don't you?" I said I did. "Well, if you get expelled you can't graduate, and if you don't graduate you can't go to college. That's the bottom line. Now get outa here, and I'll see you when I see you. If I see you." I said I appreciated his measures. "Oh hey, any time," he laughed: "my pleasure." I left his office laughing. We always cracked each other up.

But I was also laughing at my good fortune. I could stay out of school for as long as I pleased? I could hardly believe it. I drove straight downtown to Central High and, figuring everyone would know him, asked a student passing through the otherwise vacant entry hall where I might find Johnny Nilson. I was right. He told me the floor and the area of that floor where Johnny should be. (Note: Our high schools were large. Central occupied an entire city block and, like Will Rogers, had four floors.) I had a smoke in the nearest bathroom until I heard the bell, then stepped out into the now crowded corridor where I quickly found Johnny.

"Jay! What the hell are you doin' here?"

"I just got suspended, and it's a beautiful day, so I came down here to git you so we can rejoice and be glad in it."

"Jay. Are you suggestin' I cut school?"

"It'd be a cryin' shame to waste such a fine day, John. A sacrilege."

"Why, by God, Jay, when you put it that way..." and off we went to Ft. Gibson Lake where we put the day to good use fishing and drinking beer.

That night I told Mom about my suspension and what I had done to earn it. "Indefinite?" she asked.

"That's the deal," I said.

Next morning she called Hipsher, and after a little back-and-forth she said, "Okay, then, Mr. Hipsher, indefinite it is." She hung up and said to me, "One thing, Jeffrey: don't you dare get in any trouble while you're staying out of school—do you understand?"

I replied, "Yes ma'am," because I knew she meant it, which meant in turn that if I did get into any more trouble I well could wind up in reform school.

But staying out of trouble didn't mean I couldn't enjoy myself. Tuesday I persuaded Amy to call the attendance office to get herself excused from school, then we spent the day at T.U., hanging around the student union playing cards and pinball and pool in the morning, having lunch on the big patio, then watching a varsity baseball game at Harwell Field in the afternoon. I suggested we top off the day with a little romp in the hay; she said gosh, sorry, she had allergies. Wednesday and Thursday I worked at Rayco, not just to make some money, but also because I loved working there. Friday I stayed at home and read in the morning (I often skipped school just to read) and went to a movie in the afternoon. Meanwhile Mom called Hipsher twice, asking him to order me back to school. He politely insisted that going back or not was my decision and mine alone.

To Mom's considerable relief, I went back the next Monday. And I steadfastly stayed out of trouble the rest of the term because: 1) I really did want to go to college, therefore: 2) I really didn't want to get expelled, and besides: 3) there were only three weeks left in the term.

On the last day of class I ran into Hipsher. "Well, I'll be," he said, "you came back."

"Didn't you know?" I asked.

"How could I? I haven't seen you in a coon's age."

"I bet you missed me," I said.

"Don't bet much," he replied. We laughed and shook hands as he said, "Have a nice summer, Jeffrey."

"You too, Mr. Hipsher," I said, then added, "I'll be seein' you next semester."

"Yes," he sighed, "I'm sure you will."

### Shangri La

Johnny's brother Jack told Johnny and me that we should check out this new resort on Ft. Gibson Lake—the Shangri La, a swanky hotel where we could water ski on the lake, swim in the pool, eat and drink and dance in the lounge, pick up a chick, rent a room.... We got the message. The next Saturday after work Johnny and I got spiffed up—slacks, sport coats, summer fedoras—and headed for the Shangri La. The place looked good—big pool surrounded by numerous tables and chairs beneath bright umbrellas, lots of big glass windows and door walls, a large lounge looking out on the pool and, beyond the pool, the lake. And there was a trio playing. But the music was lame, and the room was occupied by a bunch of middle-aged couples quietly eating. No one was dancing.

It must be too early for the real action, we agreed, so, not wanting to blow our stash on hotel food, we drove back to the nearest town, Waggoner, and stopped at a bar where we ate hamburgers, drank beer, played some shuffleboard, and made the acquaintance of a short, muscular, tough looking guy who was sitting in a booth by himself. Called himself Red. He was home on leave from the Navy and all his old friends had moved away. We said we were fixing to go back out to the Shangri La and get laid—he could join us if he liked. He said he'd be happy to drive. He had a new Pontiac, V-eight. He told us he tended to drive fast, and he wasn't kidding: on the highway he often hit over a hundred. Back at the hotel, we found many more people in the lounge, some dancing, some eating, all drinking, and not one under the age of forty. We'd been had, by another guy named Jack. But we decided to make the best of the situation (and who knows?—maybe some girls would show up), so we sat at a table, ordered setups, and Johnny took charge.

158 *Low Crimes and Misdemeanors*

He offered drinks to the folks at adjacent tables, and took it upon himself to mix them, hand-scooping ice cubes from our bucket into glasses, pouring in two or three fingers of our bourbon, shaking a bottle of Coke or Seven-Up or soda (depending on what the good folks ordered) with a thumb over the top, holding the top over the glass and sliding his thumb aside a little to squirt the beverage into the glass like seltzer, only Johnny sometimes slid his thumb too far and the beverage spewed all over the table and the people now sitting around it enjoying the crazy kid's antics and his patter, for Johnny narrated himself in action—"He's shakin' the bottle o' Seven-Up, folks, shake rattle and roll, here's mud in your eye and fizz in your hole," and he'd squirt the fizz into a glass, and when he spewed it all over he'd holler, "Oh no! Thar she blows! In your eyes and up your nose!" and everyone would laugh and tell Johnny to try try again, practice makes perfect, if at first you don't succeed, and the like, only now they were giving him their booze and mixers to play with. By the time the trio took a break we were all smashed. Johnny went to the bandstand and over the mike invited one and all to his diving exhibition at the pool.

The water shimmered in the glow of underwater lights, which provided the only illumination in the surrounding darkness, so that the scene looked like a velvet painting by a tasteless Rembrandt. Johnny climbed up the ladder to the high board and shouted, "And now, ladies and gents, you are about to witness the first fully-clothed one-and-a-half somersault in the history of high diving! Okey-dokey, here goes! Kiss your ass and touch your toes!" and he did it, a one-and-a-half in shoes, slacks, sport coat, and fedora. When he surfaced he fetched his hat, waved it to acknowledge the laughs and cheers, and started to climb up the ladder out of the pool when he happened to turn around, then yell "Legs!" and dive back in toward the opposite side. Then I saw her, just what we had come for, a pretty teenager in a bathing suit sitting on the edge of the pool, her feet in the water. Halfway across Johnny lifted his head, again yelled "Legs!" and resumed swimming. The girl leaped up and ran away, and a man in a hotel blazer said to Red and me, "Is that young man a friend of yours?" We said yes. "Would yall mind gittin' him outa here, before someone gits hurt?" We said no and helped Johnny out of the pool, telling him we were going to Muskogee where girls—many, many girls—were waiting for us, ripe and ready for the plucking.

I got in the front seat with Red. Soaking wet, Johnny got in the back seat, curled up in a ball, and passed out. Red was doing at least a hundred when he missed a detour and we crashed through barrels and sawhorses, spinning around three or four times before coming to a stop. Red and I sat still for a moment, both of us perfectly calm, too drunk to be alarmed, and Johnny still sound asleep, too drunk to be conscious, then I said, "Looks like we just had a wreck." Red said, "Yep." We got out to have a look. The left rear wheel was buried at least a foot in sand, the left front wheel was all twisted, the left front fender was crumpled. Red got in the car and as I pushed he rocked it back and forth until we got the wheel out of the sand onto pavement. Red found he could drive it, but only twenty miles an hour. We were just sober and functional enough to realize that we should not call for a tow truck and that we should cancel our Muskogee plans, because otherwise we might wind up dealing with the law and that would not—repeat: *not*—be good. So we drove back to Waggoner, fifteen miles or so, the wheel grating against the fender the whole way.

Just outside of Waggoner Red pulled into the front yard of his grandfolks' farm house, where he was staying. We tried rousing Johnny, failed, then Red and I went in and shared the bed in his old bedroom. I fell asleep and almost instantly, it seemed, felt cold water splashing my face. I opened my eyes. Johnny. He said it was noon, time to go home. We woke up Red. He introduced us to his grandfolks, who looked like first cousins of the American Gothic couple. Red drove us to the bar where my Ford was parked, we all said goodbye, been good to know you, and Johnny and I

160        *Low Crimes and Misdemeanors*

drove back to Tulsa.

On the way he told me that he woke up waterlogged and bladderfull, stumbled out of the car that Red had parked under a big oak and started peeing on the trunk when he looked up to see this old couple sitting in rocking chairs on their porch staring at him with expressionless faces. He finished peeing, said howdy, and asked if Red and I were inside. They said yes, he walked in and found us by echo-location—following the racket our snoring made—woke us up, here we were, and wasn't Red a helluva guy, and even though we had fallen short of our destinations and objectives (as usual, I pointed out), wasn't last night a bitch? And I said was it ever.

### *A Little Night Swim*

From seventh grade I knew a girl named Darlene Owens who was about as perky and cute as a girl could be: olive skin, sparkly eyes, big smile, loads of pep, muscular, shapely, witty. I liked her so much I didn't mind that she played the accordion, a numbingly popular instrument at the time. I didn't even mind when she played "Lady of Spain," a numbingly popular tune among all the accordion players. And we got along, Darlene and I—we enjoyed each other's teasing, me about her accordion, her about my delinquencies. Yet—and don't ask why—I never asked her out.

Darlene lived in an area of newer, upscale ranch houses that surrounded a large pond, and any number of times she told me to come on over, with some friends if I'd like, and have a swim. The only catch was, the pond was private, so she had to be along. Well, a swim with Darlene was fine by me, but whenever I called no one answered the phone. Whenever we ran into each other she'd tell me to call, I'd tell her I had, she'd apologize and tell me to try again. And every once in a while I would, and every single time no one answered the phone.

This stalemate lasted for at least three years. One hot night Billy, Johnny, and I wanted to cool off with a swim, but somewhere different from McClure's. Like a pond. Like Darlene's pond. I called her—no answer. At the end of my patience, I suggested we take a dip without her, and Johnny and Billy said that under the circumstances, we should.

We drove by her house just in case she was home and for some odd reason hadn't answered the phone, but it was dark. Billy parked his car on another street. We slipped between two houses that were also dark, then stripped and slipped quietly into the pond. The water was nice and cool. Overhead the moon was down, the stars thick and bright. We dog paddled around some, careful not to disturb the silence and stillness, and for a while it was fun, like we were frogmen in enemy waters, but after a while we got bored. Across the pond was a little dock, and jutting out from the dock a little diving board. We decided the time had come to disturb the peace.

We quietly dog paddled across, pulled ourselves up the ladder at the end of the dock, then, one quickly after the other, we ran and sprang off the board and plunged into the water with loud shouts and splashing cannonballs.

Instantly two outdoor patio lights came on, and a large man in a long-sleeved white dress shirt slid open a doorwall and walked down to the dock, looking out over the pond. We silently treaded water beyond the reach of the lights. He walked to his left along the edge of the pond, and we started stealthily treading back to the other side. He walked to his right, peering into the darkness. He walked back and forth several times, some twenty, twenty-five yards, looking and looking. Finally we got to the other side, then Johnny suddenly surged out of the water splashing and yelling, "Fuck you, you chickenshit sonofabitch!" and Blam! Blam! Blam! three reports just like that, and seeing his arm raised we realized the man was shooting at Johnny—at us— with a pistol we hadn't seen he was carrying. We scrambled out of the pond, grabbed our clothes, tore ass to Billy's car, jumped in and took off, all with the hyper-speed of characters in a Mack Sennett comedy.

In the car Johnny said he could hear the bullets hit the water. We agreed that the man was a sonofabitch alright: shooting at folks for taking a dip, even though the dippers were trespassing, was disproportionate. But effective: we sure as hell weren't going there again, not without Darlene, at least.

For the sake of symmetry, Billy went back the next night and hurled a small boulder into the man's front door.

A week later I ran into Darlene in a grocery store. Studying my face and smiling, she said that some guys went swimming in her pond one night last week and got shot at. With a straight face I merely said oh. Still smiling, she added that the man who shot at them got his front door busted up the next night. I said hmmm. She said hmmm? I said hmmm. She laughed and asked if I still wanted to swim there, or if I had given up. I said I was still game. "Then call me again," she said: "someday we'll go swimming." I did, a few more times, with no luck, then I did give up, concluding that a swim with the lovely Darlene Owens just wasn't meant to be.

### *Hot Times in a Colored Town*

Oklahoma had more all-colored towns than any other state. Near Coweta there was one—Red Bird, I think it was called—a few little houses sprinkled around a white wood-frame one-room school house on one side of a dirt road and a little cinder-block bar on the other. In summer there were dances every Saturday night in the school house. I heard about them from Sonny Barnes Delojier, one of the black guys I worked with at Rayco. He urged me to come on out and join the fun. I didn't need coaxing.

Johnny and I dressed up and met Sonny there the very next Saturday night. He was a strapping, tobacco-chewing guy in his early twenties who loved to tell long tall tales in which he was a gittar-playin', blues-singin', hard-partyin', hard-lovin', head-bashin' child of the wild who not only put ordinary men in their places, he taught Chuck Berry and Bo Diddly their licks and the ladies their limits. (His colored pals said he was full of shit.) Sonny Barnes introduced Johnny and me to T.P. Smith. Turned out T.P. was the brother of Buzzy, another co-worker at Rayco. You wouldn't have known they were brothers. While Buzzy was maybe five eight and slight, T.P. was about six four and built like a tight end, and while Buzzy was intensely religious and very married with two kids, T.P. was just as intensely unreligious and very single, a man who, as he liked to say with every new drink, "Let the good times roll!" The only resemblance they bore each other was their color, a rich, chocolate-pudding brown.

Johnny and I were the only whites there, but we didn't care—it was hardly the first time we were a racial minority—and no one else cared either. We all had a fine time. The band was basic—drums, bass, sax, electric guitar—and everyone danced. Between sets many of us crossed the road and had a couple of beers, then went back to the school house. There we nipped on Jim Beam and danced some more. The party lasted until three or so in the morning.

Next Saturday Johnny and I went back, where again we met Sonny Barnes and T.P. and had just as much fun, the only difference being that this time there were several other white guys there, all teenagers. Johnny and I didn't know them. They kept to a table by themselves. They didn't dance, but they didn't come looking for trouble, and they seemed to enjoy themselves, which primarily meant, judging by appearances, getting blottoed. Johnny and I regarded them as interlopers and kept our distance.

The next Saturday Johnny couldn't make it, so I drove out by myself. There were a few more white guys I didn't know, and again, they didn't dance, didn't mingle, didn't cause any problems, but did get knee-crawling drunk.

164    *Low Crimes and Misdemeanors*

I regarded them with a degree of scorn and apprehension. Because if too many of them started coming, they could bring the law in their train. And sure enough, the next Saturday when I was in the bar with Sonny Barnes and T.P. between sets (once again Johnny couldn't make it), word spread almost as fast as thought that the highway patrol were raiding the schoolhouse. Folks were scared and angry. "Fuckin' police, why don't they just leave us alone?" they asked. "What we doin' to bother them? We mindin' our business, why don't they mind theirs?"

"We'll just stay here till they leave, Jeppey," Sonny Barnes said.

"And hope to God they don't come over here," T.P. added.

"What the hell!" I said indignantly. "We're not doin' anything!"

"*We're* not doin' anything," T.P. said. "*You* are drinkin' under age."

And Sonny observed, "Besides, since when you got to be doin' sumpn to get in trouble with the law?"

"Oh, alright," I said, and got another beer. A while later, though, I ran out of patience: the cops must have left the schoolhouse by now, and they obviously weren't going to raid the bar or they would've already, so I announced I was going back. T.P. and Sonny tried to persuade me to wait, but I was drunk beyond the power of persuasion, however reasonable.

We were walking up the steps to the schoolhouse together just as two highway patrolmen—who were white, of course—came out of the door. One of them said, "What the hell're you doin' here, Red?" and pushed me. I landed on my back in the dirt. I lurched to my feet as the other patrolman said, "Let's see your driver's license, Red."

As I was fumbling with my wallet, T.P. said, "He ain't causin' any trouble, officer."

The patrolmen didn't respond. In the beam of a metal flashlight the size of a billyclub he looked at my license.

"Seventeen, eh?" he said. "How'd you get here?"

"My car."

"We can drive him home, officer," Sonny Barnes said. "We'll take care of him."

"Where's your car?" I pointed. "Let's see it."

As I led the way, Sonny and T.P. repeated their assurances—I wasn't bothering anybody, they would drive me home—but the patrolmen paid no attention. They looked through my car, and when one of them reached under my front seat I knew I was doomed even before he pulled out my reserve pint of Jim Beam which without a word he held up for the world to see, letting the evidence speak for itself. At the sight of that bottle, T.P. and Sonny also knew I was doomed and didn't say another word. "Your keys," the other patrolman said. With sinking heart sinking lower, I handed them over. He started my car, goosed the accelerator, and through my illegal steel-pack mufflers my engine rumbled and roared. Without a word he goosed it a couple more times, letting the evidence bellow for itself, then turned off the ignition and said, "With those pipes you can't drive this even sober, Red, so we're gonna have it towed. And you're a minor who's illegally drunk and illegally in possession of whisky, so we're gonna have to tow you in as well."

"But there are guys in there," I protested, meaning the white guys, and knowing the cops knew who I meant, "who're so drunk they can't even walk!"

"Don't you worry about them," a patrolman said. "You got enough to worry about all by yourself." They each took me by an arm. "Let's go."

The patrolmen drove me downtown to the county jail, where they put me into a room with five or six other guys I happened to know. Acquaintances, not friends, but the coincidence amused us all. "Hey, Duncan, what the hell're you here for?" they asked me.

"Can't you tell?" I asked: "I'm drunk."

"And disorderly?"

"Naw, I'm a happy drunk. What the hell're yall doin

here?"

"Incitin' a riot," they said.

"Just havin' a bit o' harmless fun, you mean," I laughed.

"That's exactly what we said to the cops, but do they listen? Noooo."

We got booked and thrown into a cell together. The building was fairly new, the cell large, clean, well-lit. I lay down on one of the beds and fell asleep. Next thing I knew a jailer was saying, "Let's go, boys, let's go," as he was escorting them single file out the door. Groggy and hungover, I was last in line. "Not you, Red," he said, pushed me back into the cell, slammed the door shut, and led the boys away. Once again no radio, no TV, nothing to read, nothing to do. After a while the jailer brought me some thin oatmeal, dry toast, and weak coffee. "Hey, officer," I said as he handed me the tray through a slot in the door, "how come you let those other guys out but didn't..." I stopped because he was gone. About half an hour later he came back to pick up my dishes and we had the same one-sided incomplete conversation. After that I didn't see or hear anyone for three or four hours. Once in a while I would holler stuff like, "Hey, I want outa here! I wanta make a call, goddamnit! Yoo hoo! Is anybody fucking home?!" It's a very lonely feeling, shouting with all your might into a void. Had I been listening I might have heard in response a still, small voice, but I'll never know because I was looking for a cop, not the Lord.

Finally one walked past the cell. Applying my mother's lessons in etiquette, I said in my nicest, politest voice, "Excuse me, officer, but may I please ask you a question?"

"Your lunch will be coming soon."

"No sir, not that. I'd like to know why yall are holding me here. You let the other guys out hours ago, and their offense was much—"

"We let them out because they're minors, Red. Simple."

And I bellowed, "Because they're minors?! I'm only seventeen, goddamnit!"

"You're what?" he asked, obviously surprised.

"You heard me: seventeen. Look at my driver's license. You'll see."

"Oh shit," he said, and hurried off in the direction he had come from. Soon another cop came and took me to an office where I called Mom. She wasn't at all surprised that I was calling her from jail. As she put it, "Where else, Jeffrey?" She picked me up, and after I told her what all had happened, she told me I would have to pay for everything— the tow fee, the storage fee, the ticket, the fine. And if I got sent to reform school, so be it. "You dug yourself into this hole, you dig yourself out," she said, and I said fair enough. (What else could I say?)

Next week Mom and I saw a probation officer, a trim, short-haired guy in his thirties who was wearing a short-sleeved dress shirt and a thin tie. He told me he was putting me on probation of a modified sort: I didn't have to periodically report in, but they would be keeping tabs on me. And if I got in more trouble, I'd have a nice long vacation in reform school. Then he said, "And the first thing you can do to stay out of trouble is stay away from nigger joints."

"I'm glad you brought that up, officer," Mom said. "It worries me sick that he goes to those places."

"But there's nothing to worry about," I said.

"They're extremely dangerous," the probation officer said. "Fights, brawls, knifings, shootings—they happen all the time. I know, because we have to deal with them all the time."

"See, Jeffrey?" Mom said.

"But I've never gotten in trouble at a colored place."

"Uh, excuse me, Jeffrey," the man said, "but you're in trouble now precisely because you were in a colored place."

"No sir," I said. "I'm in trouble now because I got caught drunk, which could happen just as easy in a white joint. And I gotta tell you, I've seen more fights and bad stuff in white joints than I have in colored."

"Then you've been lucky," he said. "As for white joints, stay away from them too. You've got no business going to any kinda joints."

"I like the music. I like to dance."

"Then listen to the radio. Go to your sock hops. You understand?"

"Yes sir," I said, meaning only that I understood, not that I'd take his advice. Sock hops? He was out of his mind. I would just be more careful, that was all.

I paid the towing fee, the storage fee, the ticket for the illegal mufflers, and the fine for being a minor in possession of illegal alcohol and for being drunk and orderly (as I put it to Mom) in a public place. I don't remember the total amount, but it set me back. Way back.

The whole episode nagged at me for several years because I didn't understand why I got busted while none of the other white guys did. The patrolmen had seen how some of them were so drunk they could hardly walk or talk, so why me and not them? And then one day, apropos of nothing, it came to me, and it was so obvious I had to wonder why I hadn't seen it before: they nailed me, not because I was drunk—that was only a pretext—but because I was with, truly *with*, a couple of black guys. A kind of guilt by association. So that, ironically enough, the more T.P. and Sonny tried to help me out, the deeper they dug me in: the patrolmen would see to it that I would by God pay for being a nigger lover. So I did, but the price was worth it: Sonny and T.P. were great guys, and we had some fine times.

### Another Bust

Jim and I were aimlessly driving around one night drinking beer and talking about God, Life, and Death—when he'd had a few, Jim liked to chew on the big issues—and on

North Apache we saw a little bar with a sign saying *Archie's* standing alone with a few cars in the lot. We decided we'd like to have a couple more and pulled in. Turned out it was a colored bar. The bartender, who welcomed us warmly, was Archie himself. There were a number of colored there, plus three cute white girls who were sitting in a booth by themselves. Jim and I wound up feeding the juke box and dancing with the girls for a couple of hours. We got ideas because they liked to dirty bop. We offered to take them out for a little drive—code for a little action—but they declined. Declined *Jim*, the guy who looked like a composite of James Dean and Paul Newman! They did, however, offer to meet us there the next Saturday.

We met them there the next two or three weeks, and it was the same: we had a good time dancing, but that was all the good time they wanted. The last night we went there Jim got frustrated, I guess, because he decided he wanted to fight. He didn't care who he fought, just as long as he could have a fight. After being turned down by several patrons he was asking me if I would humor him when in walked three white boys, one of whom was Donny Gallagher, the answer to Jim's prayer. And to mine, truth be told: I didn't see the fun in fighting for the fun of it, but if I *had* to, for the sake of my reputation...

We'd known Donny for years and got along just fine, though we had never hung around with him. What marked his arrival as providential was that he was a boxer. He trained at the Y and fought in tournaments. And he accepted Jim's invitation to fight as if it were an invitation to a party: "Gosh, Jim," he said, "I'd love to." Archie told us to settle our business far far away, so, while the black folks laughed and told us to have a ball and don't no one git hurt now, all of us white kids, including the girls, piled into two cars. ("They might not wanta fuck," Jim said, "but they sure want to see a fight.")

We drove a mile or so, then turned onto a little road for a bit until I saw to the side a patch of dirt and gravel. We parked and got out of the cars, but left the motors and the lights on. In the beam of the lights Jim and Donny, who were about the same size, took off their jackets and shirts, stepped off the gravel into grassy pasture, shook hands, then began trading blows. The rest of us cheered them on, not one or the other, but both together, since this was a fight that in the soccer world is called a "friendly."

Suddenly a bunch of cops were grabbing us and yelling, "You're all under arrest! In the cars! In the cars!" They pushed us into the patrol cars they had pulled up in and parked so quietly that none of us had noticed. "Oh shit," I thought: "here we go again."

At the police station they separated us. In a tiny little office a couple of cops asked me to tell them where we'd been drinking. I wouldn't say. Then they told me that if I didn't tell them, they'd throw me in jail and throw the book at me—underage drunk and disorderly, inciting a riot. I still wouldn't say. Then they said that with my record—they had looked me up—I was prime for a year or so in reform school. If I told them, on the other hand, they would press no charges and let me go home.

I loathed ratting. According to the code I wanted to live by, the word said it all: rat, about the lowest a body could get, on a level with fucking a whore the night your wife delivers your baby. And I liked Archie, and didn't want him to get nailed for serving minors (like me) and probably lose his license and his business. But I also feared the prospect of reform school. As I saw it at that moment, it was either Archie's business or my ass, and to my everlasting shame, I took the low road and ratted to save my ass. I was no better than the snitches in Pauls Valley.

Jim's dad fetched us. On the way home he told us how stupid we were, and Jim said he'd had it with Tulsa, he was going to go to Hollywood and be a movie star, and his dad said that that was exactly what he was talking about: stupid. (By the by, Jim's dream of Hollywood proved to be a passing fancy: he never even mentioned it again, much less went there.)

Monday morning, after paying the fees for towing and storage, I got my car from the garage it had been hauled to. Monday evening Mom said, "Take a look at this," and pointed to a story in the *Tribune* about some minors who got arrested at a field where a couple of them were fighting after they had all been drinking at a bar named Archie's. Three of the youngsters were girls, it said, two of them fourteen and one only twelve, and I thought to myself, Holy shit! Fourteen! *Twelve!* None of them looked a day under sixteen.

As neutrally as possible I said, "Pretty crazy."

"Stupid, actually. You can't be too careful, Jeffrey. You ever heard of statutory rape?" I said no. She explained, I listened, and after that I was very careful. I didn't ask girls for i.d.'s, but I did ask leading questions.

### *A Politically Incorrect Occurrence at the Carolina*

Rolly was an all-conference tackle. He dearly loved football, so during the season he trained hard and stayed away from parties, drink, and tobacco. At season's end, however, he made up for lost time. Especially his senior year, because, having no plans to play in college, the last game was his last game. After that game he and Billy and I went to a wild party at someone's house where there were no parents. Beer and whisky were flowing, rock and roll was blasting from a phonograph, kids were singing and dancing and groping, some guys were occasionally scuffling, and Rolly, standing on a chair in the middle of the room, holding a fifth of Jim Beam in one hand and a cigar in the other, happily waved his arms over the mayhem like a conductor.

Toward one or two in the a.m. Rolly told me he wanted to go to the Carolina. Billy said he did too. I drove them there. We walked up the L-structured stairs to the lobby where the girls in their negligees lined up. Billy picked one and took off with her down the hallway. I thought Rolly was going to do the same, but it turned out he only had fifty cents. He asked me if he could borrow five, but I was broke, so he turned to the girls and asked if he could have fifty cents' worth of their services. "Juss some titty," he said: "all I want's to feel some titty." They looked at him in disbelief. "Okay," he begged, "juss lemme see some titty. Please! Juss a look. Juss one little look. Juss one titty!" But they weren't interested in giving him titty in any sense or number and walked back to their sitting room.

We stayed on the landing waiting for Billy. A bell rang, the girls returned, we all listened to footsteps coming up the stairs, and then onto the landing walked four dwarfs. It was obvious they were professional wrestlers—one was dressed like a cowboy, one like an Indian, one like a farmer (straw hat, bib-overalls, shit-kicker boots), and one like a turn-of-the-century eastern dandy (derby, three-piece suit, spats). Sad to say, but truth to tell, the sight of those dwarfs was funny.

I managed to refrain from laughing by telling myself that dwarfs are human, after all—they get horny just like everyone else, and these guys were on the road all the time, so where and how else could they get laid?—but Rolly was too drunk to refrain from anything. He pointed at the poor guys and laughed uproariously, whooping, bellowing, staggering around, all of which the sad-eyed dwarfs and the impassive girls and I quite properly and ridiculously pretended not to notice, until he fell down, but instead of falling on the floor in a heap, he fell on the first step and with a clattering racket of shoes and head thudding against wood he rolled down the stairs, around the bend of the L, and all the way down to the front door, laughing helplessly the entire way. I hustled after him, helped him get to his feet—he wasn't hurt, naturally, just limp from drink and laughter— and helped him out the door and to the car and into the back seat where he promptly passed out. Figuring I probably wouldn't be welcome on the landing, I waited in the car for Billy.

That was my last trip to the Carolina.

### *Oklahoma City Redux*

One weekend the winter of 1956-57, Rolly and I visited Jack. My car was on the fritz so we hitchhiked. Saturday we watched Jack wrestle, and that night we went to a bar where Rolly and I got ripped, though Jack held back, having decided to train for a change. Rolly was in such party mode that three or four times he chugged two bottles of beer at the same time. We closed the bar at two, and Jack drove us to his house where Rolly and I, sharing a bed, instantly fell asleep.

The next thing I knew, the overhead light was on and Mr. and Mrs. Walcott were rousing us out of the bed and stripping off the blankets and sheets, and Mrs. Walcott was saying, "It's alright, Rollen—it's okay, honey," and then I smelled the puke, and Mr. Walcott was helping Rolly out of the room saying, "Let's go to the bathroom and get you cleaned up, son," and Mrs. Walcott was mopping puke up off the floor, and I was mumbling incoherent apologies, and Mr. Walcott led Rolly back into the bedroom, and Mr. and Mrs. Walcott put on fresh sheets and blankets while Rolly and I both mumbled incoherent apologies, and they said, "Now now, everyone messes up now and then. Just get back to bed and sleep it off. And when you get up we'll have a nice big breakfast." Then they were gone. The door was shut, the room dark and very still. For a few minutes Rolly and I lay there, equally still. I knew what was coming and was trying to prepare rejoinders. Then it came.

"I gotta git outa here."

"No, Rolly. You gotta stay and face 'em."

"No I don't."

"They said it was okay. That everyone messes up now and then. They'll forgive you. They've already forgiven you."

"I can't face 'em."

"If you don't now, you never will, Rolly. You'll never see them again."

"I know."

"But you've known 'em for years. They've known you. You don't wanta lose that."

"You're right. I don't. But I can't face 'em."

And I knew he really couldn't. I could have in his place, but Rolly was shy, intensely shy, and I wasn't. So I said, "Okay, let's go."

"You don't have to go," he said. "You didn't puke all over the place."

"If you go, I go too," I said. "Let's go."

We dressed in the dark, crawled out of the window, and started walking toward the Turnpike. We would have hitchhiked, but there was no traffic. Coming to an all-night diner, we realized we were hungry. Between us we had fifty cents. We shared a barbecue sandwich and a Pepsi. Half-hungover, half-drunk, still hungry and suffering heartburn, we walked three or four miles before we got to the strip of motels near the turnpike. There was still no traffic, so we went into the lobby of one of the motels to rest.

In the lobby was a fountain. Suddenly Rolly said, "Money!" and was on his knees at the edge scooping up coins from the bottom. I looked around. No one else was in sight, so I joined him, but then Rolly suddenly stopped, saying, "Aw shit."

"What?"

"Look," he said, and pointed to a sign over the fountain. *March of Dimes.* Rolly started tossing the coins he'd grabbed back into the fountain.

I said, "Wait, man! We can borrow some, you know. Pay it back in Tulsa."

"We're not takin' money from crippled kids." Rolly said.

"We're *not* takin' it from crippled kids," I explained. "From here, from Tulsa, from wherever, the money all goes to headquarters, so the crippled kids git it all the same."

"We're not takin' any money from crippled kids," Rolly repeated, and as you've probably gathered by now, once Rolly had made his mind up, there was no arguing with him.

We threw the rest of the coins we'd picked up back into the fountain, went back out and got a ride from a sassy young couple who took us all the way to Tulsa, which we appreciated, but who engaged us the entire time in a conversation about college high jinks—wild frat parties, crazy sorority shindigs, beer busts, panty raids, and the like—which we ordinarily would have enjoyed but now we didn't because all we wanted to do was sleep. In Tulsa we got a ride from a woman who was more observant: seeing the shape we were in, she said, "Good Gawd almighty, you boys look like living hell," and kindly took us to our homes.

Mom looked at me, shook her head, laughed, and said, "I think you better go to bed." I happily obeyed.

As Rolly and I knew it would be, that was our last trip to Oklahoma City.

### *A Blind Date*

My senior year Mom was dating a dapper salesman I liked a lot, Lee Burner—a tall-tale teller from Louisiana who loved to cook and eat and drink, who enjoyed hearing about my escapades and who never advised me to be a good boy, only to be smart. One day Lee told me his teenage niece Emily was coming up from Houston for a visit, and would I be kind enough to take her out for an evening? I said sure and asked when. The *when* was a bummer: it was the Saturday night B.B. King was playing at the Big Ten, a night I had been looking forward to for weeks. But hey, she was Lee's niece, I had said yes, and besides, what if she turned out to be a hot chick?

But she wasn't a hot chick—she was a plain Jane built like Lee, which in a male is stocky, but in a female is

176         *Low Crimes and Misdemeanors*

dumpy. But she was Lee's niece, so I was going to show her the sort of real nice time that I ordinarily shunned: a typical high-school date. I took her to the Ritz to see a movie, then to Bishop's Restaurant for a snack. Making conversation was hard. We had no interests in common. Emily found my efforts at humor mildly amusing at best, and she made no efforts at humor herself—not one. Our small talk was punctuated by silences that were punctuated by longer silences. When we finished our coke and fries it was only like ten o'clock, far too early for a date to end, but I didn't know what to do next. Then it occurred to me. Maybe Emily would like to see B.B. King!

I decided to start subtly, indirectly, asking, "Do you like rhythm and blues, Emily?" She looked puzzled. "You know, like rock and roll. Big Joe Turner. 'Shake, Rattle, and Roll.'"

"Oh, that was Bill Haley and the Comets."

"Yeah, but they got it from Big Joe Turner. 'Honey, Hush.' 'Flip, Flop, and Fly.'"

"Oh, yeah," she said, but I could tell she didn't know Big Joe Turner from Rin Tin Tin, so I tried a title that went with a name she couldn't help but know.

"And 'Tutti Frutti,'" I said, praying she wouldn't say Pat Boone.

"Pat Boone!" she said. "That's a good one."

"But he got it from Little Richard."

"Oh yeah!" she exclaimed, and I knew I had struck a real memory. "His is a lot better."

"Funkier," I said. "He also did 'Long Tall Sally' and 'Good Golly, Miss Molly.'"

"Oh, those are great!" She was interested.

"Well, you know, Emily, there's a guy playing in town tonight who's sorta like Little Richard and Big Joe Turner."

"Really?" she said. "And he's here in town tonight?

"He sure is," I said. "Would you like to see him?"

"Oh wow, would I ever! I've never seen anyone like that. But isn't it a little late?"

"Oh, not at all. He probly won't go on till eleven-thirty or twelve."

"Wow."

"But here's the deal," I said. "B.B. King is colored."

"Well. Little Richard's colored. And Nat King Cole. Johnny Mathis. I don't care."

"Yeah," I said, "but the deal is, he's playing at a place that's colored. A big place—huge, in fact: holds maybe two thousand people—and probly at least ninety-five percent of 'em are Negroes. And tonight, with B.B. playin', it's gonna be packed. You ever been in a place like that?"

"No."

"Well, I have, quite a bit, and I've never had any trouble, but you may not want to, and I'd understand. I mean, it's kinda strange at first, being in the middle of that many Negroes, when you're not used to it."

"But you've done it?"

"Lots. And never had a lick of trouble. But if you'd feel uncomfortable, Emily, well, I understand, and it'd be best not to go."

"Oh, but I wanta go. It sounds really cool."

Suddenly I was one happy fella. It looked like I had underestimated Emily, and we were going to have a fine time after all, a Tulsa Saturday night she and I would never forget.

At the Big Ten I paid for the tickets and a table close to the stage. As I had expected, the warm-up band was still going at it. I ordered setups, persuaded Emily to try Seven-Up with a tad of bourbon, and mixed myself a strong one. Fifteen minutes later the band stopped and the leader said B.B. would begin shortly and he was going to play without letup until he had worn us all out. I couldn't believe my luck: a jam session no less! Then Emily leaned toward me and whispered, "I have to leave."

"You have to leave? Why?"

"I'm scared."

"Scared o' what?"

She whispered, "This place. I've never... all these...

colored."

"But nothin's happening. Do you see any trouble? Anyone fightin'? Anyone even fussin'? Everyone's just havin' a good time."

"I'm sorry. I just didn't realize... I'm scared." Her voice was shaking, her lip quivering, her eyes beginning to well up. "I can't stay here. Please take me home."

Well, hell, what was I going to do? She was Lee's niece, and I loved Lee, and she was terrified, so I took her home. On the way we didn't speak. I walked her to the door, and she said she was sorry. Reminding myself that she was Lee's niece, and that it wasn't the end of the world after all, I philosophically shrugged and said it was okay. And if that had been the end of the story, it kinda would have been.

But it wasn't the end of the story. A week or so later Lee was over to the house for dinner, and he took me aside and said, "Jeff, I understand you took Emily to a nigger joint." Well, now I *really* felt betrayed, and furious, but I refrained from outburst and simply explained what had happened instead. When I finished Lee said, "Well, son, I have to say your story makes more sense than hers. But you still shouldn't have taken her to a nigger joint." I told him, in all honesty, that I was sorry. I just didn't say why I was sorry—that besides disappointing him, I had spent forty bucks for a lousy time with a girl who was, as far as I was concerned, even though she was Lee's niece, a piece of shit.

But I have to admit, it did turn out to be a Tulsa Saturday night I never forgot.

### An Adversary

His name was Rudy Simmons. I became acquainted with him in the second semester of junior year, in a required course called Personal Hygiene. The purpose of the course was not to teach us how to bathe and brush our teeth, but how to avoid the perils of drink, drugs, and sex. We had to watch a lot of movies that were laughable. Like one in which a girl took a drink of whiskey and instantly passed out on the front seat of a car. We knew better: during class we sometimes snuck drinks of vodka out of those little bottles they sell on airplanes, and we weren't passing out.

The teacher, Bessie Hiett, was a thin, nervous woman who, in a shaky, querulous voice, pleaded for cooperation. Command was beyond her. I felt sorry for her, but that didn't keep me, nor several others, from walking all over her. As we saw it, if she let us, she deserved it.

Rudy was one of the walkers. Sort of. A couple of times he brought the little bottles to class himself, and he made a point of helping pass them around surreptitiously, but, I noticed, he never drank any himself. He'd suggest we carp and complain when she gave out exams or assigned homework, but when the time came, I noticed that he remained silent. Once Mrs. Hiett threatened to send a classmate out of the room if he didn't hush up, and Rudy whispered, "If she kicks Pat out, we all go, right?" We said right. A few minutes later Pat mouthed off and she ordered him out of the room. He and I stood up and looked at our fellow trouble-makers. They were sitting at their desks, staring down. In the hall Pat and I cursed them every one, but especially Rudy, since he was the one who had suggested the walkout. I decided I hated him.

I had never hated anyone before, had never nursed the desire for a long time to beat a particular party to a pulp. But I didn't feel I could beat him up without some provocation, some pretext. So for the rest of that semester, and during the next semester, and on into the spring semester of my senior year, I looked for an opportunity. When I saw Rudy in the halls, at games, at dances, at parties, I'd hang around in his vicinity, often make conversation, always hoping he'd say or do something that could even remotely be deemed fightworthy, but he didn't. It was as if he knew what I was up to and was always on his guard.

One Saturday night there was a large party in a club

in a strip mall out on Eleventh. I watched Rudy being the life of the party. He was smoking without inhaling, making a big to-do over the whiskey he was pretending to drink while loudly encouraging others to drink up, slug it down, let's get plowed, and boasting about how he'd arranged to get laid before the night was over—all the horse-hockey I despised, but as usual nothing egregious enough to justify a fight. I decided that if I was going to beat him up I might as well do it now, on general principles, since it was clear I was never going to get the specific grounds I wanted. I told him I'd like to talk to him outside, in the back parking lot. He said sure. A number of guys—friends of his, friends of mine, acquaintances of us both—wondering like Rudy what was up, followed us. In the middle of the lot I stopped and said, "Rudy, what I want to say is, I think you're a chickenshit who needs to git his ass whipped."

"Why?" he said. "What'd I do?"

"You're a troublemaker."

"You should talk!"

"No no," I said, "I git in trouble; you make others git in trouble. It's time you got the shit beat outa ya, and I wanta be the one to do it, cause I hate your fuckin' guts!" I raised my fists.

He said, "Hey, wait, Jeff. Let's—"

"I been waitin' for over a year, Rudy, and I've run out of patience!"

I faked a jab, to get him to raise his fists, which he did, then I charged him swinging both fists. I don't know if any landed, but I do know he hit me in the head. It didn't hurt, but it was solid, and it surprised me. In the scenarios I'd imagined month after month, he never hit me. And now a brand-new idea crossed my mind: what if the sonofabitch beat me!

The potential for irony and humiliation was too much to bear. I charged into him head first, pushing him into the side of a car and punching his body. Almost immediately he bolted out of the parking lot, his friends taking off with him.

Disappointed, the remaining guys shrugged and said, "That's all, folks. So much for that fight. TKO. TKO?—naw, that was a forfeit." I was a little disappointed myself, but at least I had given Rudy a moral thrashing: he had run. We went back inside and, in response to questions, played down what had happened, which was easy enough—not much had happened.

The following Monday I got a summons to see Mr. Cleveland, the Dean of Boys. It was a new position instituted my senior year, and it meant I saw him when I got into trouble instead of my pal Hipsher. I didn't care much for Mr. Cleveland. Whereas Hipsher was cool, Mr. Cleveland was hearty and gung-ho, always beaming and bouncing, and he constantly told me how I was shortchanging my potential, a theme that always made me impatient and tired. Early in the second semester, though, he caught me smoking in the delivery entrance when I should have been in machine shop, and without smiling he informed me that if I got into any more trouble he would expel me, no probation, no appeals, no overs—did I understand? I understood.

Expulsion was the one and only threat that made me mind. College was a given I never questioned. I can't say why I never questioned it. I questioned everything else. Maybe because I simply couldn't disappoint Mom on that score, since I had given her so much disappointment and grief on just about every other. Maybe. Also, I'd always heard how cool college was, and hanging around T.U. as much as I did, seeing students all the time, I always thought it looked cool. Whatever the reason (or reasons), there it was, a sacred duty, and consequently I stayed out of trouble for the rest of my time in school. And as a consequence of that, damned if Mr. Cleveland didn't regard me as one of his success stories, the wayward kid he'd turned around, telling me and anyone else in the vicinity any number of times, and always with that big toothy smile of his, how proud he was of me. (Meaning yourself, I always thought.)

So, the Monday after my set-to with Rudy I got a

summons to see Mr. Cleveland. With a big smile he said, "I bet you're wondering why I've sent for you, Jeffrey." I allowed I was. "Well, it's because I've heard you got in a fight with Rudy Simmons over the weekend." Astonished and damn near panic-stricken, I wondered how he knew. Did he have informants? Spies? Could I be punished for something I did off-campus, off-hours? "Is that right?" he prompted, still smiling.

I had to say something. "Well, I don't know if I'd, I mean, it's, you know, like..."

"Well, Jeffrey, all I want to say is, I hope you did, because that sorry sonofabitch is long overdue for a beating." Again I was astonished, but still wary: was Mr. Cleveland setting me up for a confession, so he could slam me? He continued, "I've been wanting to suspend him ever since I got this job. He's an instigator. Like that basketball game out at the Pavilion, the announcer told the spectators to stay off the court, and Rudy was scurrying around telling everyone to rush on to the court after the game, and sure enough a slew of students did, and there was Rudy on the sidelines, jumping up and down, laughing. He pulls that stuff all the time. I've been watching him, hoping that just once he'll actually break some rule himself, so I can nail him. You know what I mean?"

Figuring I could answer honestly without incriminating myself, I said, "Yeah I know."

"But he never goes too far, so I've also been hoping that someone would clean his clock. And lo and behold, I hear you did." He was smiling now bigger than ever. "Did you?"

"Sorta," I said.

"Sorta?"

"It was over before it hardly started."

"What do you mean?"

"He ran."

"He ran?" Mr. Cleveland burst out laughing. "Well of course he ran, he's such a chickenshit! Oh that's rich!

Perfect!"

When he was finished laughing, I asked, "How'd you hear, Mr. Cleveland?"

"Oh, word gets around, that's all. So I want to say thanks. I appreciate it."

Once again I was surprised. "You really called me in to thank me for gittin' in a fight?"

"For that fight, you bet I did."

Beaming, he stood up and came around his desk, shook my hand, and escorted me to the door, which he opened for me, then winked and whispered, "You oughta get a medal."

Well, the man soared in my estimation. His gung-ho bounce was not phony, but for real. *He* was for real, not a rules-monger, not a goody-two-shoes, not a square, after all. So what the hell, if he wanted to regard me as one of his success stories, that was okay with me.

A few days later I heard that Rudy was telling everyone that he ran because he was afraid he'd kill me. Enraged, I told Rolly I was going to beat the living shit out of the bastard, even if I had to chase him to hell and gone to do it. And Rolly said, "C'mon, Jeff, he's not worth the trouble. Forget it." And as soon as he said it, I knew he was right. So I put aside my grievance and my hate and even vaguely forgave him, though obviously enough I didn't forget.


### Senior Week

In the spring of my senior year Mom accepted a job offer from a man in California, where the rest of the family had already moved. So I was going to get there at last!—the palms, the ocean, the beaches, the babes! (When I told Amy I was going to move there, she said she hoped I would score with those girls better than I had with her. I said I did too.) The only possible drawback, the way I saw it, was that Mom would have to leave before the semester was over and Gram would be coming back to look after Chris and me and to get the household packed for the move. Which meant that Gram would be there during senior week. For seniors, the last week of school was basically a party, both on and off campus. It was one of the few school functions, albeit unofficial, I had ever looked forward to, and I was afraid Gram might cramp my style. I had the option of disobedience, of course, but I loved her dearly and didn't want to get our new life in California together off to a bad start.

I picked her up at the airport. Right after she had descended the steps from the plane and we had hugged and kissed, she held me at arms' length and said, "Jeff, honey, I know that senior week is coming up. All I ask is that you let me know where you are."

Not sure I heard her right, I said, "Pardon?"

"You heard me," she said. "I don't care what time of night or day it is, just call and tell me where you are and give me the phone number. That's all I ask."

"That's a deal, Gram," I said. Oh, we had always been close and compatible, Gram and I, but even so I could hardly believe my luck.

All through senior week Gram proved true to her word: I went to clubs, to bars, to houses of friends and acquaintances, to houses of strangers, and whenever I arrived, three p.m. or three a.m., I called and told her the address and phone number, and she always said, "Thank you, honey. Have a good time!" And I did, except for one disappointing night when Johnny and I picked up a couple of young women in a dance club and went to their apartment where Johnny's young woman showed us nude photos of herself and my young woman resisted all my advances with a stiffness bordering on hostility. Several days later I realized they were a lesbian couple, and with that realization, whether it was true or not, I comforted my ego.

The main event on my calendar was a camp-out at Ft. Gibson Lake with Billy, Rolly, Bob Taylor, Dante Austeri, and Roy Hauer. (Three of my buddies you've read so much about couldn't make it: Jack was in Oklahoma City, Johnny was going to his high school's festivities, and Jim had joined the Marines.) Bob Taylor was a super-likeable guy I hung out with my senior year. A close friend of Dante's and Roy's, he was quite good looking in a Jimmy Darren sort of way, and he had a very good voice in an Elvis sort of way, and he could actually play a guitar, and he had a real good band, all of which made him the rock star of Will Rogers High. Fortunately, he was level-headed enough not to let stardom go to his head. On the contrary, as his almost constant ironic smile indicated, he found it amusing.

Dante was another guy I hung out with my senior year. In Tulsa in the 50's, he was an exotic specimen: in addition to his name (Dante Allegro Austeri, no less), he was short and swarthy, with a thick shock of black hair and big muscles popping out of his white tee shirt. Pecs no less. Which, to the girls' embarrassment and delight, he would flex, one at a time or both at once, and both at once in the same direction or different directions, making them jump around like a tassel-dancer's tits. He came from New Jersey, and he wrestled. His mother and father came from Sicily. His father was a professional wrestler. They lived in a trailer. Dante had us over for dinner a number of times, where we enjoyed genuine Italian cooking and Chianti and an Italian mother saying, "*Mange*, boys! *Mange, mange!*" He got us into professional wrestling matches for free, where we got to watch his dad, Tony, who was a bad guy, plus many others, including the incomparable Gorgeous George.

Dante was multi-faceted. In addition to wrestling he pulled A's in the hardest courses: chemistry, physics, trig, calculus. He sculpted an absolutely beautiful bust of his Hollywood hero, James Dean. (Along the same lines, Rolly took an art class his last semester and did one and only one painting, a fine watercolor of a stein of beer.) When he wasn't in training Dante loved to horse around and drink and go dancing.

Roy was altogether different from Bob and Dante and

186          *Low Crimes and Misdemeanors*

the rest of us—a large, soft, pigeon-toed, bookish, witty guy who wore horn-rimmed glasses that he was always pushing up the bridge of his nose with a forefinger. Roy and I were in the same rigorous college-prep English class that met on both sides of lunch hour. We often went off-campus to eat. Sometimes we got back late. A game spontaneously combusted with the teacher, Mrs. Gibson, a tiny stern-faced woman who looked like a tough version of the older Ruth Gordon, and who *was* tough, *so* tough—she piled on the work and the discipline—that her nickname was Mighty Madge, but who also had, Roy and I discovered, a fine sense of play: if we could come up with an excuse she enjoyed, she would not mark us tardy. Roy and I would spend lunch cooking up a story. We rescued a stranded kitty ("How sweet of you," she said.), accidentally ran over a dog ("Oh, that's a pity."), saved a damsel in distress ("You've got to do better than that, boys: there are no damsels anymore."), stopped a robbery in progress ("That's better, but not credible."), tended an accident victim until the ambulance arrived ("A gold star in your crowns."), quelled an incipient riot ("Quelled? Incipient? Very good, boys!"), and the like.

Speaking of Roy and Dante...

## *A Digression*

Because I flunked the second semester of sophomore English, my academic advisor, Miss pain-in-the-ass Edwina Calhoun, said I had to take it again, even though I was passing the toughest English course in the history of secondary education. I suggested other courses that were more rigorous—*I* did, the guy who preferred skating by—but, a bureaucratic fundamentalist to the core, she declared I had flunked the second semester of sophomore English, therefore I had to re-take the second semester of sophomore English.

The class was remarkably boring, the students amazingly immature. (Oh the difference between sophomores and seniors!) The only thing that made it bearable was a couple of girls. They were friends. Both were dark and curvaceous, and both had bright smiles that revealed very straight, very white teeth plus lips a guy would love to lick and nibble on. One, Sandra, was a stranger to me; the other, Maria, I already knew. She was Dante's sister.

Maria was exhibiting puberty at its best—she had become full-figured without overdoing it—which meant to Papa Tony and Brother Dante, they being old-school Italian, that she needed to be guarded against predatory teenage males. When Tony was out on the road, which was most of the time, Dante was Maria's primary guardian. Mess with her, you'd have to mess with him. So I regarded Maria as strictly off-limits. Her friend Sandra, however, was fair game. I was thinking of asking her out, but wanted to find out first if she was dating anyone.

One day at lunch I mentioned my interest to Roy. He snorted Coke through his nose, then told me that he knew Sandra was available and was in fact quite interested in me. I asked how he knew. He asked if I could keep a secret. I said sure. He said that if I betrayed this secret, his death would be on my hands. I said he could trust me. He hesitated, then said he had been dating Maria on the sly for two months. I said holy shit. He said no shit. I said no lie? He said God's truth. I said holy shit.

Knowing I would feel compromised whatever I did, I not only kept Roy's secret, I even conspired with him, by double-dating one night, him with Maria, me with Sandra. Roy and I picked them up in my car at a branch library where they were supposed to be studying together. We drove around until we found a field with a hill from the top of which we could look at the city lights while we necked. But we never got to the top because I got stuck, which I should have anticipated. The spring of 1957 was exceptionally wet and wild: many thunder storms, tornados in the vicinity every two or three nights, inches and feet of rain. It stood to reason that the field would be deep in mud, but I wasn't operating on reason, and in a few moments we were stuck hubcap deep in mud. I tried to rock my way free, spinning the wheels in first then reverse then first then reverse a few times, but to no avail.

Sandra began sobbing. Her parents were going to kill her if they found out she was marooned in a car with a guy out in the boonies instead of studying in the library like she said she was. Maria and Roy reassured her that we would get back in time, and I thought how ironic it was that they, who really had something to worry about, were comforting this self-centered hysterical twit who could walk back to town for all I cared, even though she was gorgeous. Finally Roy and I got out of the car, told Maria how to shift gears and rock the car—Sandra was utterly incapacitated by now, a quivering jelly curled up fetal fashion in the front seat—and, with Roy and me pushing and getting thoroughly splattered with mud, the three of us managed to get the car free. I drove the girls back to the library well before Sandra's parents were to pick her up. She apologized, and knew by my silence that I didn't accept it.

On the way to the bar (Roy and I needed a drink) I told Roy how impressed I was by Maria's grace under pressure, and by her concern for someone besides herself. "Yeah, I know," he said: "too bad she's Dante's sister. That was our last date. We can't deal with the guilt any more." When he said that, I thought even more highly of Maria. And of Roy. Class acts, both of them.

Next Monday Sandra dropped a note on my desk, profusely apologizing, hoping I would give her another chance. I didn't.

## Senior Week Continued: the Camp-Out

On a late Saturday afternoon six of us—Billy, Rolly, Bob, Dante, Roy, and I—stashed our gear, including a pony keg, in the trunk of my Ford, squeezed into the car, and took off. It was going to be a sentimental journey for the usual reasons—we were all graduating and going our separate ways. Rolly and Roy were going into the Navy, Bob was going to tour with his band, Dante was going to Oklahoma University on a wrestling scholarship, Billy was going to Oklahoma State, I was going to California. What made this party an even bigger tear-jerker was Roy. He was going into the Navy under duress, the duress coming from his father, who insisted that while Roy was obviously college material, he needed a couple years' military experience first to finish growing up, and since Dad had the power of the purse, Roy had signed up, even though he really didn't want to. So Roy was maudlin even before we left town, and as we passed a fifth of vodka around—even Billy was imbibing now, though carefully—Roy got maudliner.

By the time we got to Broken Arrow, maybe fifteen minutes away, he was singing "I've Got a Feeling Called the Blues" and "So Long, It's Been Good to Know You." Ten minutes later he was telling us what a chickenshit he was to let his father browbeat him the way he did. Some fifteen minutes later he was blubbering how we were the bess fuckin' buddies a fella c'd ever wish for, 'n' when he was swabbin' decks in the middle some fuckin' ocean're other, he's gonna miss us, by God. Ten minutes later we had to stop, haul him out of the car, and hold him on top of an embankment to keep him from rolling down it as he puked his guts out. By the time we got to the lake, a little over an hour after leaving Tulsa, he had the dry heaves.

We parked on top of a hill, laid Roy in the back seat to sleep the night out, and found a decent camp site fifty yards down the hill. We made a couple trips back and forth carrying the gear down to the site while Roy snored and drooled. We tapped the keg (first things first), built a fire, laid out our sleeping bags, and were just getting around to heating some beans and roasting some hot dogs when it started. *It* being my horn honking, over and over, and Roy bellowing my name. We tried to ignore the racket, but after fifteen minutes we conceded that Roy was driving us nuts. But, we agreed, he couldn't keep it up. He had to pass out. But he did keep it up, for at least thirty minutes more. Finally we walked up to the car. "Whadda you want, Roy?" I asked.

"Take me home," he pleaded.

"You don't wanta go home, buddy," Dante said.

"Yes I do," Roy whined.

"You don't wanta face your dad in your condition," Bob said.

"I don' care," Roy cried, "I juss wanna go home. Take me home, Jeff. Please!"

"I'm not gonna mess up our party by drivin' clear back to Tulsa and then clear back to here just because you feel like shit, Roy," I said.

"Please?"

"No, goddamnit!" Billy yelled. "Now shut the fuck up and go to sleep!"

The five of us walked back down to our camp site, poured ourselves a beer, and marveled yet again that anyone could get so drunk as fast as Roy did—almost as fast as the kids in the warning films we saw in Personal Hygiene. We marveled even more that anyone could pass out and within half an hour come back to and want to face his heavy-handed old man. Then it started again, the honking and bellowing, until we couldn't stand it any more and returned to the car.

"Take me home, Jeff! Please!

Rolly offered to knock him out—one punch to the chin, he said, was all it would take—but given Roy's powers of recuperation, I decided to take him home instead. The others offered to come along, but I said Roy needed the back seat to lay his big fat ass on, and there was no reason they couldn't party, so the four of them went back down the hill to the camp site and I drove Roy home. "Ah, Jeff, you're th' bess buddy fella c'd ask for, I really 'preciate this, the bess—"

"Shut up, shitface," I said, and he did. He slept all the way back to Tulsa, until we got to his house, when he suddenly reached over my shoulder and honked the horn, lurched out of the car, staggered up the walk to his front steps and onto the porch and up to his dad, a big man standing in the doorway, and fell into his arms. I drove back to the lake and the boys, and we spent the rest of the night drinking and reminiscing about our days in high school and speculating about our futures out of high school. And talking about Roy, about whom we came to a consensus: his dad was right. A guy who couldn't handle his liquor any better than that had a lot of growing up to do.

### *Conclusion*

For some reason, I was selected to read the last will and testament at our final assembly. Well, not for some reason. The simple fact that a ne'er-do-well in an undeserved cap and gown (to complete my minor in machine shop I asked the teacher to please give me a D, even though I hadn't made one thing the entire school year, and when he hesitated I pointed out that if he didn't I wouldn't graduate, and would have to take his class again, and he didn't want that, did he?, and he said God no and gave me the D)—the simple fact that it was an anti-student who got up to read the document was good for a laugh. And besides, I could put on some act.

After the assembly, Rolly, Billy, and I repaired to the Buccaneer for lunch. After lunch we walked out the back door and saw an unattended beer truck wide open for the pickin', so we picked a couple of cases, threw them in the trunk of my car, drove to my house, iced down the bottles in a washtub on the back porch, called Johnny, and the four of us, remembering Jack and Jim, had our last party, only this one wasn't about graduation, just good-bye.

The next day Gram, Chris, and I loaded up my Ford. We checked the house—the house that Gram and Grad built, that Mom then Chris and I grew up in—to make sure we hadn't overlooked anything. Except for a lot of memories, we found nothing. We opened the car door for our dog Jack, who jumped in and lay down in his favorite spot—the floor on the driver's side, under the pedals. We pushed and pulled him over to the passenger side, then got in ourselves. We sat there in the driveway for a minute or two, not speaking, just thinking, feeling. Then Gram said, "Okay, honey, let's go." I started the motor and gunned it a couple of times, making a loud mellow uproar through my illegal mufflers as a way of saying goodbye to the neighbors, then shifted to reverse, backed out of the driveway for the last time, shifted to first, depressed the accelerator, released the clutch, and headed west.